21 Days to *Helping* Your Child Learn

Books in the 21-Day Series

A Proven Plan for Beginning New Habits

21 Days to *Helping* Your Child Learn

Cheri Fuller

Series Editor
Dan Benson

Zondervan Publishing House
Grand Rapids, Michigan

A Division of HarperCollinsPublishers

21 Days to Helping Your Child Learn
Copyright © 1998 by Cheri Fuller

Requests for information should be addressed to:

ZondervanPublishingHouse
Grand Rapids, Michigan 49530

ISBN: 0-310-21748-2

Published in association with the literary agency of Alive Communications, Inc., 1465 Kelly Johnson Blvd. #320, Colorado Springs, CO 80920

Interior design by Sherri L. Hoffman

Printed in the United States of America

98 99 00 01 02 03 04 /❖ DC/ 10 9 8 7 6 5 4 3 2 1

CONTENTS

PREFACE

Welcome to 21 Days to Helping Your Child Learn!

Bill and Martha's middle schooler, Brad, used to be the most curious kid on the block—asking questions, doing projects, and exploring every waking hour. But they hear from his fifth-grade teachers that he's bored in class and the only question he asks is, "How much longer until school's out?" Consequently, he's making grades well below his ability level. These parents are baffled because the bright child they knew has "shut down" to learning. How can Bill and Martha help improve Brad's attitude and achievement at school?

Vicki decided to home school her children, but finds it's not easy motivating her kids, ages 11, 9, and 7, to be eager learners every day. They seem to get bogged down in the reams of worksheets, and Vicki is always looking for the best way to help her children learn. Some days she gets downright frustrated with them. She wants to be an encouraging motivator, not a drill sergeant. What can this mom do to help her kids enjoy learning?

Beverly's son, Jason, has had problems with reading since first grade, and now in the third grade he's beginning to have struggles in math and social studies, too. Jason procrastinates with homework and often "forgets" to bring his books home. Since school's such a struggle for them both, Beverly wonders how they're going to make it another nine years until he graduates from high school. What can she do, she wonders, to turn this situation around and help Jason enjoy learning?

Maybe you identify with Vicki, Beverly, or Martha and Bill. Or maybe your child hasn't started to school yet, but you want to help him or her get a great start on learning. Or your child may be a high-energy kid who not only has trouble staying seated in the classroom but also getting all his work done. Or she's a perfectionist whose learning gets derailed by too much emphasis on "making the grade." Maybe, like many parents I know, two of your children do well in school and one seems turned in the other direction.

You've come to the right book.

21 DAYS TO HELPING YOUR CHILD LEARN

The good news is that, as a parent, you can have a terrifically positive impact on your children's education. What you do and how you're involved in your children's learning has more influence on their attitude and achievement than anything any other person does. Your home environment can become one that supports the learning process. And by taking the step-by-step methods I'm going to share in this book, your children will become more motivated, more curious, more aware of their interests, more organized about schoolwork, and will *enjoy* learning more. You can help your children develop academic skills that will take them the distance in this marathon of education.

Human performance specialists tell us that it takes twenty-one days to form a new habit. For example, if your finances usually are in chaos and you meet with a financial counselor who suggests better ways of handling your money, you can form new, healthy financial habits just by applying these techniques for twenty-one days. Apply the same principle to running or other exercise. Complete a daily exercise regime for twenty-one days and you'll not only be healthier, more energetic, and "hooked" on exercise, but if you stopped after those three weeks, you'd probably miss the daily exercise routine.

Studies have shown the same twenty-one-day principle applies to other areas of life that need a positive change: eating habits, smoking, relationships, and even parenting. The twenty-one-day approach builds momentum that actually propels you in the direction you want to go. This dynamic principle is the foundation for the *21 Days* series—practical steps to positive life change—and it's the cornerstone of this book, *21 Days to Helping Your Child Learn*.

Over and over I've seen that when parents get involved in their children's learning, the results are dynamic. Studies of children who succeed in learning and school reveal parents who are actively engaged in helping their kids throughout their school years. When parents show an interest in school by asking questions and reinforcing learning at home, students get more motivated and achieve higher marks.

As a former teacher and a mother of three grown children, with over twenty-five years of experience in both camps, I've worked with parents like Bill and Martha, Beverly, and Vicki and spoken to hundreds more. I've given them ideas to support their children's learning, turn around negative attitudes about learning, and help their kids get the most out of the school experience, whether they are being educated at home or at a public or private school. I've seen parents themselves get motivated and recharged with new ideas and strategies that make a huge difference in their children's learning.

GUIDING KIDS ALONG A POSITIVE PATH

In this book, I'll guide you along a twenty-one-day journey with strategies, activities, and creative solutions to common problems that hinder children's learning. You'll also gain some new perspectives about learning that will help *you* be a lifelong learner. As you'll see, a love of learning is contagious, just like the chicken pox or stomach virus that ran through your family— and kids "catch it" (the love and excitement of learning, that is) from parents who *enjoy learning*. In the process, if you follow the twenty-one-day plan, your child will

- take more initiative in school and home tasks,
- become a more active learner,
- be a more curious learner,
- be more motivated about reading, writing, and learning,
- be able to bounce back from setbacks and overcome obstacles.

You'll also save, over the long haul, hundreds of hours of hassle over homework. And, perhaps most important of all, you'll be helping your children enter into the great adventure of learning and develop their potential to the fullest.

Each day's lesson in *21 Days to Helping Your Child Learn* is brief, simple, and to the point, sprinkled with a little humor and stories that illustrate the points. I know you're a busy parent and don't have time to read fifty pages of text before you get to the ideas that will help your child, so I'm going to provide straightforward and doable steps any parent can take. Get your paper, pen, and highlighter out—and be ready for action! Stay with me, and at the end of twenty-one days, you *and* your child will be encouraged and ready to tackle the next challenge in school and life. Happy reading, parenting, and learning!

Have High Expectations

*Expecting the best will motivate your
child for maximum learning.*

Did you know that a child's mental capacity is amazing? Within the first four years of life, the child's brain grows to two thirds of its adult size, growing at a faster rate than in his or her whole lifetime. This expansion carries with it the potential to go way beyond what report cards and IQ tests can reveal. Children are born motivated, and they learn more in the first five years when they aren't sitting in classrooms doing assignments than they do in the rest of their lives!

Corporate trainers spend huge sums to get business executives to think divergently and creatively. Children think that way naturally. A good example of kids' bright thinking occurred in a teacher's classroom one day. The teacher had just presented a science unit on magnets to her first grade class. The class had done demonstrations and experiments with magnets, talked about magnets, and finished a worksheet on magnetism. Then in a follow-up test, one question read: "My name starts with *M*, has six letters, and I pick up things. What am I?"

Guess what the kids answered? Half the class gave the word *MOTHER!*

Maybe you've read in newspapers about U.S. students having a poor showing in international achievement tests, but let me encourage you with the fact that *America is blessed with smart children!* There's no shortage of intelligence. In fact, each child—including yours—has the potential to do something better than 10,000 other people *if* that child's talents and intelligence are discovered and developed.

But there *is* a short supply of something—belief and hope and high expectations for our children. Generally American parents and teachers do not expect excellence from children, either academically or morally. There are also too many negative labels—such as LD, ADD, and ED—which produce a downward spiral. A negative label leads to *low expectations,* which lead to *less effort* and thus *lower achievement* and *less learning.*

Today I want to raise your expectations about your children because *your* expectations are powerful and they significantly impact your child's behavior, achievement, and learning! What we expect from children is usually what we get.

THE POWER OF HIGH EXPECTATIONS

Children who succeed and overcome obstacles usually have one thing in common—they each have at least one person in their life who has high expectations for them and who provides structure for their dreams. Let me share an example with you: Until Shavar Jeffries was eight years old, he was shuttled among family members. When he was eleven, his stepfather murdered his mother. Shavar was definitely an at-risk child.

He and his sister had to move in with their grandmother, Nancy, who worked nights as a prison guard so Shavar could attend a private Catholic school, since they lived in a bad area. The grandmother had high expectations for her grandson's behavior and learning, insisted on homework and reading, and believed that Shavar could achieve. She preached to him that the reward for good grades isn't money or things but the satisfaction of learning itself.

An A student throughout his secondary schooling and college, this young man, who had a high chance of failing in elementary school, graduated from Duke University with honors and at age twenty-one is in law school. Shavar had inner drive, but his grandma believed in him and provided structure. For that, he'll always be grateful.[1]

Billy also experienced the power of high expectations. As a freshman in high school, he wanted desperately to play football. Although he practiced with the team every day, he rarely got to play because Billy was short, overweight, and so slow that he was nicknamed "Turtle" by his teammates. He didn't look like a football player, and he couldn't run like one.

But Billy's dad had high hopes for him and saw more potential in his son than everybody else did. One day, Billy's dad talked with Coach Mitchell. He told the coach that he believed it was important to draw out the best in every player in order to help each player develop his potential. Billy's dad knew his son didn't look like a great football player. But he tried to envision what Billy would look like in a few years … when he was a senior … after he had grown and developed with good coaching and guidance.

He said, "Coach, can you see Billy with an all-American jersey covering his broad shoulders and narrow waist?" That conversation changed Coach Mitchell. He began seeing people as they might be, not as they were or are … to see people's strengths rather than focusing on their weaknesses.

In the next four years, Coach Mitchell spent extra time with Billy, all the while picturing him with that all-American football jersey. And you know what? By the time Billy was a senior, he'd become a star football player *and* an all-American![2]

THE SELF-FULFILLING PROPHECY

Good football coaches operate on the understanding that if they expect a player to do well, usually he will. If, however, they expect or predict a poor performance, they are likely to get it. As parents we find the same thing is true: When we expect our children to live up to certain standards and let them know what we expect, they are likely to measure up.

Psychologists call this impact of expectations "The Theory of the Self-Fulfilling Prophecy," and much research proves that it works. A professor went into a ghetto area of San Francisco where schoolchildren were nonachievers and poor students. At random he picked twenty-four students and divided them into two groups. He assigned twelve of these children to two teachers, telling them that the children had tremendous potential.

He assigned the other twelve children to two other teachers, telling them that their students lacked any real potential and it would be difficult to accomplish anything with them. The researcher gave each group a series of identical instructional exercises.

Six months later, he returned to check on results. The children whose teachers had been told to expect good things were doing spectacular work. Almost all of them had raised their achievement test scores in math and language. In contrast, the children in the other group were still unmotivated, had difficulty learning, and their achievement had actually decreased.[3]

Children of almost any age will live up to—or down to—their parents' and teachers' expectations. They need to hear clear boundaries and expectations (instead of conflicting messages from parents) about how they are to act and what is acceptable and unacceptable behavior. We know from many studies that kids remain loyal to parental expectations. If your children hear positive expectations—that they will do well, that they can meet daily challenges, that they will enjoy learning and go on to college—then they will do better in the classroom. As Norman Vincent Peale said, "When expectancy turns the key, great things will happen."[4]

Here are some ways *today* to set positive expectations:

1. Think, what are my expectations for my child? Write down what you expect in different areas—family relationships, homework, chores, reading—and communicate these to your child.

2. List what your child is good at: skills, talents, aptitudes, and interests.

3. Take into consideration your child's capabilities and age so that expectations are reasonable enough to be met. Otherwise, if expectations are always unattainable (like insisting every school assignment gets a perfect 100 or that your children become a star in every sport they play), kids get discouraged.

4. Look for opportunities in the course of everyday life to share your positive expectations with your children. Give them a visual picture of how far they can go with effort and work. Tell your child: "You have a wonderful ability to listen and counsel your friends. You could really help people someday," or "You have such a servant's heart. God can really use those who've learned to help and serve others!"

5. With gentleness and love, hold your children accountable for your expectations and help them set goals when progress needs to be made. Then as they meet and exceed expectations, affirm their efforts and your confidence in

them by giving a "snapshot" of their behavior: "You said you'd be home at seven o'clock, and you are. That's what I call punctuality!"

6. Never write off as failures children who are late-bloomers or who aren't "test smart," but instead have other forms of intelligence and talent. Avoid throwing cold water on their dreams and hopes by saying, "You couldn't do that. . . ." Hopes and dreams keep our motor revving and keep us motivated about life. What makes the difference in late-bloomers who bloom or underachievers who turn around is that they had someone who believed in them and didn't give up on them!

LESSON OF THE DAY

Expect the best and believe in your child.
Communicate your high hopes and great
expectations, not just today but every day.

DAY 2

Boosting Your Child's Curiosity

Curiosity is a vital building block in learning. Here's how to help your child become a curious learner.

Picture a kindergarten class. The teacher asks a question and a flurry of little hands wave in the air amid calls of "Pick me! I know!" Then, as the students turn the tables, asking the teacher questions, hands again go back up. Now picture a seventh grade class. When the teacher asks a question, how many hands wave eagerly? Odds are, not many.

Young children are extremely curious and love to explore and learn new things (remember when your three-year-old asked questions incessantly, like—Why is that worm fuzzy? Why doesn't the sun fall down out of the sky?). Research shows that as children get older, their innate curiosity seems to wane and by the time they get to junior high, they ask few questions beyond "How long 'til lunch break?"

Yet curiosity is *vital* to learning. In fact, many experts say curiosity may be the most important factor for children's brain development and success in reading, writing, science—all the many academic tasks they have at school. Schools and even the business community rank a person's ability to question as much more important than memorizing and retrieving information by rote. If curiosity is encouraged and children are given plenty of opportunities for questioning, all kids can remain curious thinkers throughout their lives. How can you encourage and even boost your child's curiosity?

DID CURIOSITY "KILL THE CAT"?

The old saying "Curiosity killed the cat" implies that somehow wondering and questioning are a bit dangerous or negative. Not so! In fact, the opposite is true. The most motivated learners and achievers tend to be inquisitive about a great many things, from the nature of a tiny insect to how a spacecraft works. Curiosity (the desire for knowledge about something, an eagerness for information) is a very important component of motivation and enthusiasm for learning. In fact, if curiosity dies, motivation to learn wanes. We need to do all we can to keep the lights of curiosity burning in children.

One of the best ways to learn anything is by asking questions. When your child asks a question, here are some positive ways to respond that will *boost* rather than *bust* that inquisitiveness:

- *If your child asks* a question you don't know the answer to, such as, "Why don't I see double when I've got two eyes?" ask what your child thinks—because children are glad to tell their ideas and they are encouraged to then ask even more questions. Sometimes they aren't wanting the answer from parents as much as they want to see if you're interested!

  You can say, "What an interesting question" or "I wonder where we could find out about that," and then jot the question on an index card so the next time you and your child are near a library, you can search out a book that explores the subject.

- *If possible, suggest an activity or experiment* that would help your children discover an answer on their own rather than giving a pat answer. This encourages further exploration and discovery. For example, if your daughter asks how many legs a spider has, help her find one in the backyard and count legs. Or you could check out the bug populations with your son and have him compare the difference between a spider and an insect (eight legs versus six legs).
- *Take time for talk*. Children from families where there is a great deal of conversation and discussion of issues tend to be better thinkers and readers and more curious learners. When we ask our children open-ended questions (in which there are no right or wrong answers), it stretches their minds and imaginations.

Dr. Jane Healy calls these questions "playful ponderings":

- What if you had a magic paintbrush that would make whatever you painted come alive. What would you paint?
- How many things can you think of to do with a balloon?
- If you could talk to animals, what would you want to ask them?[1]

ARE YOU A CURIOUS LEARNER?

Perhaps the best way you can encourage curiosity in your children is to be a curious learner yourself—reading with them about things they and you are interested in, wondering (even out loud, with a comment like "Wow, look at the color of that sunset tonight! I wonder why it's more red than last night") about things in the world around you, going on outings, and having discussions with your kids about what you see and experience.

When you *model curiosity*, your children realize that it's valuable to wonder and discover, and it encourages them to be inquisitive and follow their interests.

A good example of the power of this kind of modeling is Blair, a geologist I know, who often took his six-year-old daughter Melissa on nature walks. He'd collected rocks throughout his childhood and adulthood and it was a natural thing to cart his daughter along. He also collected small animal bones that he reassembled with glue to re-create the animals' skeletons. (I know that sounds like a strange hobby, but to each his own.)

Melissa began her own rock collection with agates, fossils, aquamarine, and other minerals, and even her own collection of small animal bones. This little girl had the most interesting assortment of "Show and Tell" material you can imagine to take to school and share with her classmates, including a porcupine head. Like father, like daughter! In the process, she learned even as a child to enjoy observing her surroundings wherever she goes—whether the pet shop or the nature trail in the woods—then to look up information about her latest find in a science book or encyclopedia.

PREPARE FOR DISCOVERY

You can help your child to be ready for exploring or short expeditions, just as Blair did. Let me encourage you to plan a nature walk or expedition to a local park with your kids within the next week. Fill a backpack with the following and take it along:

- A magnifying glass for observing in more detail. When you and your child are near a flower garden, for example, you can say, "Have you ever really looked inside a flower?" as you peer in a flower with the magnifying glass. Then give a little gasp and comment on what you see. Usually your child will want to take a look because your curiosity is a key motivator.

- An empty paper towel roll for a closer look at everyday things. It can be cut in half for a more convenient size for smaller children. The paper tube limits and focuses children's vision so they can concentrate and see things they've never noticed before—tiny creatures and growing things in the grass, a little worm in a hole in the ground.
- A "critter jar," a plastic container fitted with a mesh lid to let in air.
- Old plastic tubs with snap tops for storing "treasures" found along the way—different shapes and colors of leaves, rocks, and fossils.
- A sturdy old spoon for digging.

After collecting rocks, wildflowers, leaves, or whatever other interesting things the field or park offered, when you get home compare your "finds" with a nature handbook to help your child identify them. Handbooks on different types of birds, flowers, shells, and stars are great—easy to read but not too simple for the child who wants a basic primer on nature. This can open up all kinds of conversation and ideas for future exploration with your child.

You can turn your child's questions, your outings, and shared reading into golden opportunities for learning.

LESSON OF THE DAY

*Your child will learn much more
if you fan the flame of curiosity.*

DAY 3

Teach Your Child to Study Smarter

Children who know how to use their strengths and "learn in style" become more active learners.

Have you ever needed to learn a large amount of material for a test and you weren't quite sure how best to study and, in fact, began feeling overwhelmed by the quantity of information? Or have you ever tried to use a computer when you didn't know the operating procedures to make it run properly and do what you needed? Then you've experienced what many students experience every day in their education—frustration!

Any of us who have worked with children know that they learn and think in different ways. Some love to work independently; others like to work in groups. Some like structure and directions on how to do something. Other children like to figure it out for themselves. Too often, instead of tapping into the way children think and process information best, we expect them all to learn the same way.

STRATEGIES AND SKILLS

On a cool October evening I stood in the school stadium and watched as a line of players in navy-and-white football jerseys stood watching their teammates on the field. The team ran a play; linemen blocked them. A pass was thrown but was knocked out of bounds. On the next play, the quarterback ran for a few yards. Then it was fourth down, with eight yards to go. The offensive team ran to the sidelines to confer with their coach.

I knew the coach wouldn't have sent the players out on the field without giving them strategies and having them practice those skills all during the week. They'd worked on their game plan ahead of time. They had rehearsed the plan and practiced the plays numerous times.

Each player had specific strategies for *his* position that maximized his own personal strengths: The quarterback developed his skills in passing, handing off the ball, and running; the kicker, short and slight of build, got his kicking down so that field goals were made; the big linemen had specific blocking assignments.

We as parents can prepare our children for learning just as coaches prepare their players—with strategies and a game plan so they can learn anything they need to learn, in any class or subject.

LEARNING IN STYLE

Today you're going to discover a concept that can have a powerful, positive effect on your child's learning: I call it "learning in style." There are several different theories floating around about children's learning styles. But rather than confuse you, I want to simplify it for you. My personal experience as a teacher and parent has convinced me that there are three basic ways people take in and process information; these are called "learning modalities."

As I explain in my book *Unlocking Your Child's Learning Potential*,[1] some students learn best by seeing (reading, studying pictures and diagrams). I call them *Lookers*. It's just as though they have copy machines in their minds that help them remember spelling words and other information after studying them for only a few minutes. Lookers notice details and usually are good navigators who can find their way around even in a new location because they remember landmarks.

Talkers are very verbal and are good at listening and following oral directions from parents and teachers. It's as if they have high-quality tape recorders in their brains. Talkers usually are social kids who like to work with others in groups and can express their feelings and ideas with ease.

Talkers tend to say spelling words and other material aloud when trying to learn them. If they don't understand something, they readily ask questions or ask a classmate for help. They need to not only see information but to hear it and say it, perhaps several times, for maximum understanding and retention.

Movers have more energy than most children and tend to try everything out by doing and touching. That's also how they learn best—by a hands-on approach. Movers often shine on the athletic field—it's as though they have computers in their brains timing their movements and coordination. But they may get fidgety if they have to sit for long periods and usually get bored if all they do in class time is worksheets and pencil-and-paper assignments.

Movers have a harder time remembering oral directions, and they need a lot of physical affection to perform their best. They are active, bright kids who can become achievers and motivated learners if someone shows them how to harness their strengths.

Which type of learner is your child? Maybe your child is a combination of two styles. Think about these three styles as being like channels on a television set. Your child can receive information on several channels (through looking, talking/listening, or moving, as described above), but usually one channel comes in more clearly. Reflect on the last time you saw your child learning something important. What helped turn the lightbulb on, when your child said, "I get it!" What learning style, or channel, helps your child the most when studying and learning information?

FROM FAILURE TO SUCCESS

Here's how "learning in style" can turn failure into success. Nathan's mom brought him over to consult with me because he was a bright twelve-year-old, but was making a D in Spanish, a C in English, and an F in history. She wondered if I could do anything to help.

As Nathan and I talked, I asked him about his own style of taking in and remembering information. It seemed clear to me that he had Talker and Mover strengths, so I showed him how to use these "channels" to boost his learning. I demonstrated how he could use a tape recorder and blank tapes to make study tapes in Spanish and to memorize vocabulary words for English tests. I then told him that he could listen to the tapes with earphones while he jogged or played basketball in the driveway.

I suggested that in preparation for a history test on Fridays, Nathan teach the material to his brothers, using a big whiteboard instead of just gazing passively at the textbook. I encouraged him to learn keyboarding skills so he could use his home computer to write most of his reports and papers for school (since he had poor handwriting). In addition, I showed him how to break big tasks—like a 200-page book he had to read or a research paper—into manageable bites.

After assuring Nathan that "learning in style" would actually increase his free time and mean he would be grounded less often for poor report cards, he went home and tried the strategies. What was the outcome? By the end of the nine weeks, Nathan brought his history grade up to a B. After he used a tape recorder to study on a daily basis, his performance in Spanish class came up two letter grades. And when an autobiography was due in his English course, Nathan had it ready ahead of time—a fifteen-page story of his life that he wrote and printed using a computer.

Like tools and jumper cables in the trunk of your car that can help you get out of a tough spot on the road, finding ways for your child to study and learn that match your child's style of thinking can make a big difference.

LOOKER STUDY STRATEGIES

If your children have Looker tendencies, show them one of the following ways to tackle homework and studying:

- When events and their dates need to be learned for a history test, encourage your child to make an Illustrated Time Line, where the dates are written above a simple stick-figure illustration or picture of the event. Pictures and graphic illustrations can help your "Looker" child understand and recall what is learned.
- Make study cards out of bright-colored index cards to help your children learn material in just about any subject—math, science, foreign language, and social studies. In geography, for example, write the state on one side of the card and the capital on the other. Your child can review the cards and gradually put the ones that are memorized in a different stack until they're all in the memorized group.
- Highlight in three or four colors to categorize information: For example, to learn parts of speech, use a green highlighter

to indicate nouns, yellow for verbs, blue for adjectives, and pink for adverbs.

TALKER STUDY STRATEGIES

If your child learns best by talking and listening, use some of the following ways to study and learn new material:

- Make information to be learned into a poem or rhyme.
- Before writing a report, have your child dictate the best ideas into a tape recorder, play it back, then write the first draft. A fill-in-the-blanks study tape also can be helpful. To make the tape, the student asks a question into the microphone, waits five or more seconds, and then goes on to the next question, and so on, all the way through the material. The child can then play the tape and try to say the answer after each question.
- Study with a partner or group. They can discuss the material, debate issues, and then pick questions for a practice test they can take and score.

MOVER STUDY STRATEGIES

Movers learn best by hands-on experiences. If you are blessed with a Mover, use some of the following learning methods and watch your child shine:

- Direct, concrete experiences like lab experiments, field trips, and role-playing help movers learn more.
- Get a blackboard and challenge your child to teach *you* (or siblings) the material that needs to be learned.
- Help your child create a board game with the information to be learned. Make a spinner, use a cardboard playing board, add some playing pieces, and then learn while having fun.

- If there are abstract concepts to be learned, do a demonstration. For example, to explain fractions, cut a piece of bread in sections or a pizza in pieces. Use beans, small toy cars, or any kind of manipulatives.

Whatever your children's learning style, encourage them to make their own list of "Things I Can Do When I Study"—the strategies that make up their playbook to use on the "field" or in the classroom when there is new or difficult information to learn. Then watch as enthusiasm for learning builds.

LESSON OF THE DAY

Students will enjoy learning and learn more if they discover how to use their individual strengths.

DAY 4

Cultivate Conversation

Since learning revolves around listening, talking, and reading, children who become good communicators keep an edge in the classroom.

Cultivate conversation? *My child chatters all the time*, you may be thinking. How does that relate to school success? Actually, the development of language skills through the listening and talking that goes on in family conversation is one of the most important building blocks of learning. In fact, the better that kids are at using spoken language, the more successful they are in learning to read and write and the better they will do on aptitude and achievement tests in high school.

When communication lines between parent and child are open, motivation is significantly boosted. Research shows that kids who excel on mental tests and in schoolwork are more likely to come from homes where there is a great deal of open communication. When parents and children are interested in each other and their activities so that kids feel safe to share ideas and feelings, intellectual growth is enhanced.

You see, every mental skill—math, music, logical thinking, emotion, and, today's topic, language—has a critical period called a "learning window" when the gates of the mind are wide open and ready for optimum development. The "learning window," or readiness for learning language, extends from birth to ten years of age.[1]

During these vital years the foundation is built for all the speaking, reading, thinking, and writing abilities your children will draw from for the rest of life. But don't worry if your child is older than ten; it's never too late to start. Although the early years are prime time for language-learning, research shows that the necessary connections in the brain are available all through childhood and adolescence—even to old age if people stay active and pursue their interests.

In addition, when kids have good conversation skills, their problem-solving and listening skills, their ability to pay attention, and their school grades improve.

So what does this information mean for you as a parent? It means that language learning begins at *home* and that you will continue throughout your children's growing-up years to play a key role in their language development. Although we know that children develop vital listening and language skills through engaging in frequent conversation with adults, most parents don't utilize the many opportunities they have to talk with their children. According to recent surveys, American moms spend only eight to fifteen minutes a day talking with or explaining things to their children, and dads spend even less time in conversation with them.

Let's look today at some ways you can build your child's language skills by capitalizing on dinner table conversation, talking during the course of the day, playing games, and following directions.

DINNER TABLE UNIVERSITY

Did you know that one of the best (and least expensive) means of growing a child who loves to learn is through dinner table conversation? It's such a rich source of learning that internationally known speaker and author Leo Buscaglia said his dad's practice of having each child in the family share something at the evening meal that he or she had learned that day was the educational technique that had the most impact on his motivation and achievement. His father was an immigrant from Italy who only attended school through the fifth grade, yet he passed on a love of learning to his children through their "Dinner Table University."

"Without being aware of it, our family was growing together, sharing experiences, and participating in one another's education. And by looking at us, listening to us, respecting our input, affirming our value, giving us a sense of dignity, Papa was our most influential teacher," Buscaglia said.[2]

You can build your child's intelligence and language skills more at the family dinner table than with all the high-tech computer games and enrichment activities that could be devised at school. Try these tips at your dinner table this week:

- Turn off the TV and turn on the talk. It's hard to carry on a conversation and watch a sitcom, so eliminate the distraction of the television and enjoy conversation.
- Avoid negative, unpleasant family business such as handing out punishment for yesterday's misbehavior, hashing over low grades, or nagging about problems. Instead, create an attitude of gratitude and begin the meal by talking about the blessings, surprises, and happy things of each person's day.
- Encourage your children to become involved in the conversation, to participate and speak up in discussions. Swap stories. Talk about what each is reading. Ask them questions

such as, "What did you learn today in the electricity experiment?" or "What was the best about your day? The most frustrating?" Stir opinions and spark a lively debate about current issues in the news by sharing an interesting article clipped from a newspaper. Make even the younger members of the family feel a part of the discussion. Instead of interrupting, encourage listening and respect for each other's opinions and ideas, even if they don't agree.

- Brainstorm answers to creative questions kids wonder about, such as "Why did God create mosquitoes?" or "If God turned off all the electricity at once all over the world, who would be the person to decide what time it is?"

TALK IS CHEAP

Take advantage of other times to talk about people, events, and things of interest in your child's everyday life. You can talk with your child at home while digging in the garden, cooking, or folding clothes, and in peaceful moments when the lights are out at bedtime and thoughts bubble up that seem to be buried the rest of the day. Talk together in the car while driving to and from school. Point out signs to reinforce letters and words your child is learning. Converse while gazing together at the stars in the night sky and when swinging at the park.

With young children, even babies, talk lovingly and gently, but avoid baby talk. When you point out the bird flying by the window, explain to your little one what the bird is doing and use correct names for things. Talk about the nutritious food you're serving at lunchtime: "Here are three apple pieces for you—one, two, three. This is your orange juice."

Be specific with your language, especially when giving directions, so your child will hear and clearly understand words for objects and actions. For example, instead of saying, "Bring your things here," you might say, "Please bring me your socks and shoes and we'll put them on and go outside." Discuss what you just saw on TV and what you're going to do tomorrow, what your child is playing with and curious about.

You'll not only be building important conversational skills in your child but will build a close relationship and thus prevent many problems. "Shared time, talk, and someone to listen is the best antidote for many of the fears and difficulties children and teenagers face," a wise counselor once said.

CHUTES AND LADDERS, GAMES AND DIRECTIONS

One of our children's favorite games when they were young was "Chutes and Ladders." As they twirled the spinner and moved up or down the chutes and ladders on the colorful game board, they were painlessly reinforcing language, counting, memory, and many other skills while at the same time talking about what was on their minds between turns.

When playing a game, whether it's an indoor board game or an outdoor game, kids tend to relax and many spontaneous conversations will start.

Games also give kids a chance to read and follow directions, which transfers to the classroom. Get out a board game from the closet or playroom, dust it off, and play it with your child regularly. You'll be boosting your child's language and listening skills. Let "game time," rather than more television time, be the reward for finishing homework. And on a day when you're too busy, have an older sibling or friend play games with your child.

Here are some suggested games and the skills children develop:

- Scrabble (Scrabble Alphabet Game, Scrabble for Juniors): Spelling, language, vocabulary building

- Monopoly: Planning, problem solving, math, language
- Memory Game (See p. 93): Memory skills and visual discrimination, language skills
- Scattergories: Language, classification skills, vocabulary
- Card games, from Go Fish to Crazy Eights and Hearts: Counting, categorizing, reasoning and logic, memory, calculating probabilities, developing strategies, language
- Word games like I Spy and Categories that you can play in the car, or the old Simon Says game we spent hours playing as kids, build lots of skills: Language, following directions, paying attention, and observation

Make good conversations a regular part of every day at your house and, while you are having fun playing, talking, and listening, you'll be helping your child to love learning!

=================================== LESSON OF THE DAY

*Use dinner times and family experiences
to cultivate interesting conversations
with your kids.*

DAY 5

Help Your Child Become an Expert on a Topic

Spark your children's interest in learning by plugging into each one's center of learning excitement.

When children have their own "Expert Territory" or topic they know more about than anyone else in the family or classroom, their motivation for learning accelerates. In addition, this area of expertise can build self-esteem and help a child overcome obstacles—even seemingly impossible ones. This is a painless and effective way to help a child love to learn because we're plugging into something the child wants to know!

Today we're going to focus on finding your child's center of learning excitement (what the child is *most* interested in) and then capitalizing on it.

Just as a picture is worth a thousand words, a story can tell volumes about not only the benefits of today's lesson but also how to apply it. Let me tell you about a little boy I know named Brian. When Brian was born, he was diagnosed with Williams syndrome, a genetic condition like Down syndrome that causes heart problems, motor and coordination difficulties, and mental retardation.

In spite of the negative picture doctors painted of Brian's future, his parents began to read to him daily, beginning on his first birthday. For more than five years they never missed a night of reading, with hopes that their son would not only learn to read someday but would also love books as they did. But by age seven, in spite of lots of phonics and reading instruction at the special-education school he attended, Brian still didn't know the letters of the alphabet.

He wasn't interested in the books at school or at home and made little progress in reading. The teachers advised the parents not to worry, just to lower their expectations and accept the fact that Brian might not ever learn to read.

Still, his mom didn't give up. Instead, she looked for what interested him the most and focused on that. One Saturday when they were driving their car through the car wash, Brian begged to go through it again . . . and again, and again. He asked questions about how the car wash worked, and then he wanted to get out and ask questions of the car wash owner. Soon his favorite Saturday activity became a visit to a new car wash rather than a trip to the zoo or park.

When a local car wash owner noticed Brian's interest, he gave Brian one of the trade magazines of the industry. Brian's mom started reading *Professional Car Washing* to him at bedtime, and his interest in reading skyrocketed. Car wash magazines that he received from owners became his favorite possessions (he eventually received complimentary subscriptions to *three* car wash magazines). One night he said, "I want to be able to read that magazine like you can, Mom."

This may sound like strange reading for an eight-year-old boy, but the car wash material hit Brian's center of learning excitement—what he was most interested in. That was his mom's cue. She made big, colorful flashcards with simple words like *soap*, *enter*, *exit*, *car wash*, and *free*, and placed them around the house. Brian began to learn them. After mastering the easy ones, he learned more advanced words like *automatic*, *spot free rinse,* and even *conveyorized belt system!*

Before long, Brian was putting the words together to make sentences and was eventually able to read car wash magazines by himself. Today, at fourteen, this young man—who educators said probably wouldn't learn to read—is an avid bookworm and a regular at the local library, reading on a seventh grade level. He goes to sleep each night with a pile of his current books stacked beside him.

Even more amazing is how Brian's "expert territory" opened doors for him: At only eleven years of age, he delivered the keynote address to 6,000 adults at the International Car Wash Association's annual convention in Las Vegas and met for hours with operators and manufacturers to discuss things like the new car-dryer called "The Stripper" and the high-tech Laserwash 4000. That was the first of several all-expense paid trips for his family, opportunities for speaking, and further learning for Brian. As a result, he has many friends all over the United States who have a similar interest in the car wash business, and this bona fide teenage car wash whiz carries on a lively e-mail correspondence with them via computer.

DISCOVERING YOUR CHILD'S SPECIAL INTERESTS

When Brian's parents discovered his interest in car washes and tapped into it, it helped him learn to read and it opened doors for speaking, new relationships, computer skills, and gave him a host of other benefits, including a tremendous boost to his self-esteem. In fact, his dream is to someday own a car wash business, which his mom hopes could also serve as a place to hire and train mentally handicapped people.

Just as Brian's parents found the key to the high hopes they had for him even though he was challenged, you, too, can discover the key to realizing the hopes and dreams you have for your child. If you discover and tap into your child's interests, you will unlock the door to learning and enjoyment for your child. From my many years of working with children of all ages, I've found that every child is interested in *something*. It's just a matter of finding out what it is.

How can you tap into your child's center of learning excitement? First, discover your child's favorite areas of interests by:

- Asking questions.
- Listening.
- Noticing what your child takes pride in and gets excited about doing. In the process, be sure to look for what *your child* is interested in rather than what *you* want him or her to be interested in. And avoid pushing your child into the mold of what the rest of the family excels at or is interested in.

Here are some good questions to ask:

- What do you like to do?
- What are you good at?
- What do you enjoy doing most—at home and at school?
- What do you want to know more about?

The answers are *clues* to abilities and strengths you can highlight and develop. What subject causes your child's eyes to light up? If it's whales and dolphins, you could check out a few books on that subject this week. If it's art or music, think about ways in which you could integrate music-making or visual arts into your child's lifestyle to provide enrichment. Is it sports, swimming, or horses? Computers or maybe racing cars? Astronomy, Chinese culture, ballet, or karate? Whatever sparks your child's excitement, you can capitalize on that interest:

- Get a magazine subscription on the topic so your child will gain knowledge and information. There are magazines for almost every interest and hobby: *Boys' Life* for a child interested in scouting, *Cobblestone* for kids interested in American history, *Creative Kids* and *Stone Soup* for children interested in writing. *Field and Stream, Jr.* is terrific for kids interested in hunting and fishing, *Penny Power* is for young entrepreneurs interested in making and saving money, *3–2–1 Contact* is for science buffs, and *National Geographic World* is for young people who love geography and science. Check with the local library, school library, and bookstores.

  There also are books for almost any interest a child would have. Is your child crazy about sports heroes or dinosaurs? Libraries and bookstores contain scores of books on football, basketball, and other sports stars, books on prehistoric creatures, and any other topic you could think of. Reading can ignite kids' interests and help them become experts on a subject as well as suggest projects and places to write for more information.

- Connect your children to someone who can mentor and encourage them in their area of interest, especially if you know little about it. This person could be someone in your community, such as a veterinarian if your daughter thinks she'd like to be a vet, or a teacher or graphic artist if your son's interest is in that field. Your child could help the professional on a Saturday or just observe and talk about the work.

  If there is no one available locally, your child can learn from an expert on-line through a service provided by the University of Texas called "Electronic Emissary." It's a great opportunity for finding out more about a field of study and it's free!

A fourth grade girl was fascinated with Arthurian legends and, after learning all she could in a school unit and reading books in the library, still wanted to know more. So her dad found a professor in a major university who had volunteered in the "Electronic Emissary" program. Through e-mail and CD-ROMs, this expert shared information he knew about Arthurian legends with the fourth-grader.

 To find out what experts are available or to get more information, go to the Electronic Emissary website: http://www.tapr.org/emissary/.

Take outings and day trips to hands-on museums, zoos, living history museums, and other places that tap into your children's interests. Take them to live performances if they are excited about the arts and let them gaze into the orchestra pit and watch the conductor and musicians.

If you look for it, there's much learning available right in your own backyard—your city, county, and state. Most places have endless opportunities for adventure, whether it's the ocean and beach, wildlife habitats, architectural tours of skyscrapers in big cities, or stargazing events with local astronomers.

Give your children an opportunity for a specialized camp in their interest areas. Two sisters I know in junior high are going to "horse camp" to learn more about riding. Zachary and Jon, my nephews, have attended soccer camp in the summer. Zachary is also fascinated with marine life and oceanography, so last summer he went to a marine camp in South Texas. Many school districts have youth art camps, music and drama camps, and writing camps. In all these experiences, whether for one week or a month, kids can learn more about and gain new skills in their "expert territory."

- Ask about courses available at local community centers, through 4-H Clubs, universities and community colleges, YMCAs, art and science museums, and local symphony companies. Taking a course or workshop is a great chance for young people to find out more about and get hands-on experience in whatever their interest is. From calligraphy to pottery, karate to baby-sitting and swimming, there are many courses offered by qualified people in a variety of skills and interests, usually at a low fee.

Put this "expert" strategy to work this week and your child will begin to gain confidence and momentum for learning even those tasks and subjects that are difficult.

LESSON OF THE DAY

Discover and develop your children's area of greatest interest, each one's center of learning excitement.

Tap Into the Mozart Effect

How music can enhance your child's learning.

Did you know that music, especially classical music, can enhance your child's brain function and have many positive effects on mental ability and learning? That piano lessons can teach kids to reason? Besides the sheer enjoyment and delight it provides, music fortifies all the learning kids are doing at home and at school. "The Mozart Effect" refers to these positive benefits and the sort of "tuning up" of the circuits in a child's brain that music provides.

Exciting new research shows that positive musical experiences—including listening to, participating in, and studying music—enhance social, motor, and creative development. In addition, music boosts children's concentration, attention span, and memory while it strengthens visual, auditory, and language skills.

At the University of California at Irvine, neuroscientist Gordon Shaw and his researchers found that preschoolers who took keyboard and simple singing lessons for eight months boosted their IQ score on spatial tests by 46 percent. They also reported that college students who listened to a Mozart sonata for ten minutes achieved higher scores on spatial IQ tests.[1]

The benefits of music-making extend all the way to the college years because music lovers tend to be learners and achievers. A recent report by the Rockefeller Foundation showed that musical kids are more likely to get to college and be successful there. Over a two-year period, students who were enrolled in music courses scored an average of twenty to forty points higher on both the verbal and math portions of the SAT (Scholastic Aptitude Test) and that students who participate in their school orchestra or band are 52 percent more likely to go to college and graduate.[2]

EVEN BABIES LOVE BEETHOVEN

What does this mean for you and your child? That music participation and listening to classical music can significantly boost a child's achievement and aptitude for learning. You don't have to play the piano like a concert pianist and your child doesn't have to be a violin prodigy to receive the benefits of music. Today we're going to look at simple ways that you can provide a rich musical environment at home. Just as there are periods of "readiness" for developing reading and counting skills, there are critical periods for musical development. Although the early years, from birth to age nine, make up the "learning window," or optimum growth period, for musical abilities, it's never too late to start.

Today, let me encourage you to turn on the radio—not to the "Pop 40" station, but to the classical station. It costs you nothing (except a bit more electricity and a radio, which you probably already have). Perhaps classical music isn't your cup of tea or you feel you know little about it, so you may be wondering:

What's the difference between Schubert and sherbet? Why classical music?

There are lots of reasons, the most important being that the complex, highly structured and nonrepetitive nature of classical music stimulates thinking and brain development. It offers the brain more "food for thought" than pop tunes. And because the notes aren't slurred in classical music as they are in most synthesized modern music, children can hear and distinguish individual tones, sounds, and even different instruments. Even babies and young children can enjoy classical music.

In addition, there is a striking similarity between the patterns or rhythms of the brain when learning is taking place and the sounds of music, especially the music of Mozart, Bach, and Beethoven and other "classical," or timeless, pieces. By the way, if you're still puzzled about Schubert and sherbet, Schubert was an Austrian composer of the Romantic period who created music in the early 1800s.

If your town or city doesn't have a classical station, cassette tapes and CDs (compact discs) of composers from the 1700s to the 1900s such as Beethoven, Vivaldi, Bach, Mozart, Schubert, Brahms, Tchaikovsky, and others can now be purchased inexpensively. I've bought classical music collections on cassette tapes for as little as $3.98 at bookstores and even less at discount stores. This music is great to play in the car or as background sound in your home while your child is studying or doing homework—since listening to classical music while learning actually enhances memory and retention.

MUSIC-MAKING

Getting your children involved in music-making can be as informal as playing a collection of kids' sing-a-long songs on a cassette recorder and encouraging them to follow the beat with rhythm instruments, or it can be as specialized as private lessons and recitals. What matters is giving your child a regular opportunity to participate in music.

Here are some different ways to help your child enjoy the benefits of becoming a music maker:

- A recorder is a simple instrument with a two-octave range that is easy to learn to play. You can find recorders at music stores and at children's toy stores and learning shops with instruction books and play-along cassette tapes. Since parents' participation is a big motivation to children learning to play an instrument, you could get an alto recorder for yourself and a soprano recorder for your child, and learn to play together (appropriate for ages six and older). Besides being a lot of fun to play, the recorder provides good practice in learning to read music.

    Keyboards, lap harps, autoharps, xylophones, and guitars are all easy to learn to play at home, and many come with "follow-the-note" song sheets, instructional videos, and booklets. Tambourines cost about $6 and slide whistles are $2.

- Celebrate music by playing musical games together. "Name That Tune" can be played in the car while traveling or doing errands. The first player hums or whistles several measures of a familiar tune while the others try to guess what it is. The player who guesses the title of the song gets to be "it" and sing or hum the next tune.

- Once a month, celebrate a composer's birthday and play the compositions (you can even check out collections of classical music from a public library). Make special memories by having Family Music Night once a week where everyone gets to perform by singing a song, reciting a poem, playing an instrument, or doing a skit.

- Show your children and their friends how to make their own rhythm instruments and play them while marching in a spontaneous neighborhood parade. Moving to the music is as important as listening to it; and kids should get up and move to fully participate. An oatmeal box becomes a drum; a homemade guitar can be created out of a shoe box using five or six rubber bands of different thicknesses around the box. You can make great percussion instruments out of sandpaper blocks. With thumbtacks, secure sandpaper strips on all sides of two blocks of thick wood and then rub the blocks together to make a scraping noise.

- Take your family to live musical performances—symphony orchestra concerts, jazz ensembles, college music concerts, and musical theater productions. Often a child gets excited about wanting to play a certain instrument after seeing it played by a musician.

- If you ever played an instrument, get it out, dust it off, and practice some favorite tunes you could teach your child. The most natural and valuable music enrichment can come from a child getting to see parents enjoy making music on their own instruments. I played the guitar growing up and my kids were thrilled whenever I'd get it out and accompany them while they sang "Old MacDonald Had a Farm" or "You Are My Sunshine."

- If your children's school offers music lessons, band, orchestra, choir, or chorus as elective courses, encourage them to take advantage of those opportunities. Church choirs and holiday productions are wonderful music events for children to participate in. Attend your local school's music performances even before your children start school and you'll be whetting their appetite to play along when they're old enough.

USE MUSIC TO MAXIMIZE HOMEWORK AND STUDY TIME

If your children enjoy music, show them how to use it while learning important information for tests. For example, help your child make up a song for memorizing the U.S. capitals and states or to learn the multiplication tables. Music aids learning and strengthens memory.

How many of us learned to say the alphabet by singing the "ABC" song? Can you remember specific verses from the Bible because they were set to music and you've sung them at church? How many TV commercial jingles do you and your kids know just from hearing them between programs?

Music is processed on the right side of the brain and language is a left-brain function. That's why when music is combined with words or information you need to memorize, it aids the listener in remembering the information and even retrieving it years later.

By enjoying listening to classical music at home, finding ways for your child to participate in music-making, and taking advantage of musical experiences and training at school and church, you'll not only grow a music lover, you will also be helping your child become a better learner and achiever.

LESSON OF THE DAY

Music will pay dividends for your child's learning, so strike up the band. Listen to good music, make music together, and help your child discover the wonderful world of sound.

Focus on the Donut, Not on the Hole

How encouraging children's efforts can spur on their learning.

During the growing-up years, especially the school years, kids have a myriad of things to learn—all the way from manners to morals, from reading to foreign language, from computers to calculus. They also have to learn to make beds, get along with siblings and classmates, negotiate on the playground, follow teachers' directions, brush their teeth without being asked, play sports and musical instruments, and carry out numerous other tasks. All the skills and information they need aren't easily gained; some take months or years of practice, and some skills are extremely difficult for certain children to master.

What do all kids need as they run this long marathon we call schooling? Buckets of encouragement! Success in any skill comes from hard work, and that takes time. That's why children need a great deal of encouragement along the way.

Unfortunately, since most of us parents want our children to improve things like messy rooms, report cards, and homework assignments, we tend to see all their mistakes up close and do more correcting and criticizing than encouraging.

As I've talked with school counselors around the country and observed families, I've found that children who are unmotivated or underachieving usually have parents who use negative techniques to get performance. They focus on the *hole* (what their child is failing at or not doing well) instead of on the donut.

Such parents make comments like: "You're never going to be successful at the rate you're going" or "You never make the good grades your brother does." These negative "focusing on the hole" strategies—overreacting to mistakes, criticizing, and withholding praise until the child has made a major accomplishment worthy of recognition—don't work, yet parents often resort to them when frustrated or upset with their child's performance.

FOCUS ON THE DONUT

Today, if you can catch the concept of "focusing on the donut instead of on the hole" in your interactions with your child, and begin to apply it, you'll build a positive sense of self-worth, provide a sense of security and acceptance, and help your child learn and develop confidence to tackle whatever challenges are ahead.

What do I mean by "focusing on the donut"? That means focusing on your child's *efforts*, not just on the performance or grade. It means emphasizing and affirming the *process* of learning something ("You really worked hard at reading *Treasure Island* and outlining the book report"). It means highlighting progress instead of just results: "You got 80 on your math test this week. That's *five points* more than last week's test. Hooray!"

instead of "You only made a ninety on the spelling test? What words did you miss to lose ten points?"

It also means giving your child positive, encouraging little snapshots of progress in different areas—conduct, academic work, relationships, responsibility. ("You said you'd take out the garbage every day this week, and you did. That's what I call *responsibility!*) If you look for something to commend, *you'll find that your child's attitude and effort—and ability to learn—will improve significantly.*

NOTES IN LUNCHBOXES AND UNDER THE BEDROOM DOOR

A good way to focus on the donut, besides your spoken words, is with written notes. Whether it's a lunchbox note, a little yellow sticky note on her bathroom mirror, or a note slipped under your teen's bedroom door, a single positive comment written down can make a huge difference. With a note, you can express praise and appreciation or show your support—all the while focusing on that donut and thus giving your children the vital encouragement they need to learn and grow.

A note doesn't have to be fancy or long. Be genuine. Make it short and specific, and your child's spirits will be lifted, even after a setback at school or a hard day at sports practice.

"An ounce of praise can accomplish more than a ton of fault-finding," John Drescher, a pastor and father of five, once said.[1] We can always find things to find fault with, because kids are works in progress, just as we are. But encouragement to children is what the sun is to flowers—it's vital and necessary if they are going to grow and bloom.

It doesn't mean we have to profusely praise everything our kids do, but it does help to recognize the steps they've completed or the effort they've put into a task. You could say, "I like how you've made a list of what you need for your science project. Now let's go to the hobby shop today and get the materials so you can start." Don't wait till the project is finished to say something positive. It's better to tell your daughter how well she's playing the "Tarantella" instead of waiting to offer praise until she's mastered enough to perform at Carnegie Hall.

Encouraging words can also be expressed for what your child *is* instead of just what your child *does*. Word pictures do a wonderful job of conveying the good qualities we see developing. For example, my friend Joanna praised her young daughter Rachel for the caring way she tended to her pets. "You're just like a mother bird with her baby birds, Rachel; you take such good care of Hugo [their pup] and Kitty." With encouragement like this over the years, Rachel has grown into a teen who shows considerable care and kindness toward her friends, siblings, and cousins (and she still loves to take care of a new kitten or puppy).

GETTING A BIG PICTURE ON GRADES

What can I do when I'm disappointed in my child's report card or my child has failed a test? you may be wondering. How can I encourage instead of discourage my child? Since grades are usually a mixture of test scores, homework assignments, reports, and projects, they can be significant indicators of what your child has learned and remembered. They may help point to a learning problem or a gap in knowledge and skills. Grades are also factors that contribute to awards, scholarships, and, later on, to college admission, so they can make parents happy or frustrated.

But let's get some perspective. Although most of us parents are proud when our kids make high scores and receive scholastic awards, there is really only a small correlation between academic achievement and success in the real world. I'm sure you know many adults who are extremely successful in their careers and yet had less than stellar report cards. Einstein, Edison, Churchill, and many others were high achievers in life yet did poorly in school. As important as grades are, they aren't the only indicator of a student's potential.

The next time your children bring home disappointing test grades or report cards, ask yourself some equally important questions: What are they learning? Are they being challenged? Are they making enough progress to do the reading, work the math problems, think critically, and handle the course material for their grade level? Are they learning how to study? Are they interested in a topic or excited about learning anything new?

When a low score or dismal report card does come home, here are some ways you can respond while still focusing on the "donut":

- After talking with your child, schedule a parent-teacher conference to creatively look for solutions and enlist the teachers' input and cooperation.
- Avoid bribing or paying for grades (or withholding allowance for poor grades). I know you may not agree with this suggestion, and I have had students who were offered new puppies, a vacation trip, money, and even a car to make good grades, but I don't advise it as a motivational strategy. If you start paying for grades in the early years, it gets expensive in high school when the stakes are higher! And in the long run, it tends to diminish students' intrinsic motivation or their sense that *learning is valuable and useful for its own sake*.
- Help your child set some realistic goals for the next lap of learning. Brainstorm together on changes to make in study methods, personal organization, and classroom seating that could make a positive difference.

Start today to find something to encourage your child about. What can you say about the "donut," or what your child is trying to do? In what area has there been improvement or progress, however small? What good character quality do you see that you could affirm? Children who are cherished for who they are and encouraged for their small steps in the right direction, who know that God made them for a purpose, and that while they are growing and learning, parents are focusing on the positive instead of the negative, develop a sense of security, optimism, and confidence that helps them make the most of every learning opportunity.

LESSON OF THE DAY

Look for the promising, positive things your child is doing. Highlight those efforts and keep focusing on that donut, not on the hole!

Teach Optimism

An optimistic attitude is a key to unlocking your child's potential.

Nine-year-old Meghan started having trouble in math class when the teacher started presenting division problems. One night her mom saw her struggling to do her division homework. "I'll just never get this! I'm terrible at math!" Meghan moaned.

As much as her mother tried to help, Meghan was convinced she couldn't figure out the problems, so she finally threw her book down, gave up, and went to bed.

Have any of your children ever felt so frustrated that they wanted to throw in the towel? Or developed a negative attitude about a certain school subject and tuned out instruction? Researchers such as Dr. Martin Seligman are finding that one of the keys to learning and facing many of the challenges in school is an optimistic attitude.[1]

Optimism enables a person to overcome failure, to keep trying, and to develop a plan of action for tackling a task or assignment. While some people seem to be inherently more optimistic than others, optimism can be learned. Even children who tend to be negative, pessimistic thinkers can develop a more positive view of life and their own abilities. And since all us are going to blow it sometimes, learning to bounce back from failure is vital.

In fact, learning to not be flattened by failure is part of the pathway to achieving anything. I love what an outstanding young Harvard student, Lana Israel, said about how her parents' influence contributed to her success. "This intense feeling of encouragement provided us with an atmosphere conducive to achievement—an atmosphere that made it all right to take risks and to fail, and thus an atmosphere that allowed us to succeed."[2] Lana at age twenty is already the author of two books and was named Britain's 1994 Brain of the Year.

FACING FAILURE WITH OPTIMISM

How can you teach your child optimism? That's the focus for today's lesson. And in the process of discovering ways to help your child become more optimistic, you may just find that some of your own negative thinking—about your job, the future, or your failures—will turn around.

First, look at how *you* view failures and mistakes. Children need to know that failure is not the worst thing in the world and that it isn't defeat until you quit trying. One of the main ways children learn that is from how their parents react to their kids' mistakes. When we overreact to mistakes and get upset when they don't win in sports or they fail in some area, children start fearing failure. A fear of failure actually breeds failure.

However, if we help kids see that a mistake can be an opportunity to learn, that fear melts away. If children understand that much useful information—such as what *doesn't* work or what to try next—can be gained, they will relish difficult challenges instead of avoiding them and choosing easy tasks.

The next time your child is down in the dumps about a mistake, tell your child how scientists fail their way to success, like Thomas Edison's 5,000 experiments that flubbed before he developed the lightbulb, or all the failed attempts Jonas Salk had before he discovered the right polio vaccine that stopped a tragic worldwide epidemic.

Read your child stories about people who kept trying in spite of obstacles and failures so your child can see that "If at first you don't succeed, you're in good company!" Michael Jordan admits he has failed countless times to make a crucial shot in a basketball game, yet he is one of the all-time greatest basketball players in America.

Even great leaders have failed. Dwight Eisenhower, thirty-fourth president of the United States, was rejected three times for command positions in the military before being appointed Supreme Commander in 1942. Harry Truman, our thirty-third president, opened a hat and shirt shop at age thirty-five that went bankrupt after two years. He worked for fifteen years to pay off the debt. Abraham Lincoln, who faced numerous tragedies and was defeated several times in congressional elections, later became the sixteenth president of the United States.

Be on the lookout for other historical or modern-day heroes in the news who have come back from setbacks and triumphed against all odds. As you share these stories and model and encourage a "comeback" instead of a "give up" attitude, you'll be helping your child learn to bounce back from failure.

DIVIDE AND CONQUER

Sometimes children are pessimistic and think negatively about a task because they're overwhelmed by how big it looks. Reading a two-hundred-page book can look insurmountable to a middle-school student. Finding the answers to one hundred division problems can also be daunting. You can build confidence and optimism that it *is* possible to accomplish a tough task if it's divided into manageable bites.

For example, get out the calendar and divide the number of book pages by the number of days until the "due date" for reading the book. Divide a research paper assignment into tasks to do one week at a time. In this way, the task appears more doable, optimism grows, and the job gets done.

FAILURE IS JUST TEMPORARY

Remember what Winston Churchill said about failure: "Success is never final. Failure is seldom fatal. It's courage that counts." That's worth passing on to your kids, encouraging them to see that almost any failure or setback can be temporary and changeable.[3] Children who think pessimistically about their failure on a test often have thoughts such as: "I'm going to flunk this course ... I probably won't pass ninth grade ... and there's no way I'll get into college ... and I'll probably become a bag lady and be homeless."

Thinking negatively about their chances on the next challenge or test isn't productive. A pessimistic outlook only causes kids to put out less effort, and their performance spirals downward.

Feeling sad for a few minutes is fine, but instead of dwelling on "the worst that could happen" scenario or thoughts about "I'm a loser," help your child see that using a different way of studying—like starting five days before the exam instead of trying to cram everything into the night before, or getting some tutoring—can help overcome this failure. Lovingly encourage your child to ask, "What can I learn from this mistake?" when one is made. Encourage your child to avoid blaming other people ("It's just my teacher's fault. She did a lousy job of teaching algebra, and that's why I don't understand it") or blaming "bad luck" or chance. Instead, remind your child that hard work will make a difference.

You also can stir up optimism by reminding your child of some things he or she *has* done well or succeeded in, such as, "Remember when you had a hard time with your multiplication tables but you persevered and found a way to memorize them, pulling a strong B on the test?" We tend to forget our past successes when faced with a failure or discouragement, and recalling the little victories and realizing how far we've come builds courage to try again.

Tomorrow we will look at a companion of optimism—perseverance—which can help your child become a successful learner. In the meantime, remember: If at first you don't succeed in a challenge you are facing at your job or at home, you're not alone. Pull out an old encyclopedia or book and read with your child about one of these "Comeback Heroes": Albert Einstein, Enrico Caruso, Dwight L. Moody, Winston Churchill, Dave Dravecky, Louis Pasteur, and Henry Ford.

LESSON OF THE DAY

An optimistic attitude is a vital factor in learning. Help your child bounce back from failure and you'll be paving the way for future learning and achievement.

DAY 9

Teach Perseverance

The importance of a "stick-to-it" attitude in the learning process.

One of the greatest assets you can give your child is helping him or her to learn the value or character quality of *perseverance*. We all experience failures and mistakes, whether trying to learn a new subject like chemistry or learning the skills needed in a challenging new job. One factor that determines how well we face those challenges and are able to muster the courage to keep trying is how much perseverance we have.

Like many values—respect, responsibility, and honesty, for instance—perseverance profoundly affects a child's learning and success, not only in school but in life. The best place to learn these values is at home, and *you* are the best person to transfer them to your children so they become internalized and a part of your children's character.

Perseverance is the kind of stick-to-it commitment and determination that keeps someone from throwing in the towel even when a situation or task gets difficult. You can be super smart, but without exercising the steady perseverance and persistence it takes to overcome setbacks and obstacles, you can't accomplish anything in the real world or learn much of anything.

LET YOUR WALK MATCH YOUR TALK

One of the most powerful ways to teach perseverance to your child is to line up your actions—what you're doing in real life—with your words. Isn't it amazing how much our children learn from us just by observing how we live and handle life's challenges?

That's why telling your child, "I know your soccer team has lost all its games so far this season, but that's no reason to miss games or quit"—while your child sees you keep working on a problem until you find a solution—makes a powerful impact on your child's understanding of the value of perseverance.

However, if you say, "Don't quit the team," when he's bored with a sport, but you drop out of the choir midway into Christmas program rehearsals because you don't like the director, it's doubtful your child will think it's important to be persistent when the going gets rough. This applies to any value you're trying to teach your child. If you want your teenage son to develop a servant's heart, take him along when you serve at the soup kitchen for the homeless. If you want your children to be caring to others, nurture them with care and loving concern. They may listen to our words, but what they really imitate is our actions.

GROWING PUMPKINS AND PERSEVERANCE

Kids need real-life practice, activities that give them opportunities to persevere (in other words, some difficult tasks that they might get tired of and want to quit). If everything they do is easy and fast, they will have few chances to persist against obstacles. Developing any value is much like building muscles—it takes regular workouts or daily training. Here are a few "workouts" that will develop perseverance in your child:

- *Gardening* is a great activity for perseverance-building. Try growing pumpkins or watermelons from seeds. Two young brothers in Minnesota decided (with their grandpa's encouragement) to grow blackberries on his farm. Grandpa provided a plot of ground and taught his grandsons what to do; they did the work and got to keep the profits. After the boys' careful and persistent care over many months, they had such a big crop of blackberries that they began selling the fruit at a stand.

- *A savings account*, to which your child adds a little money every week or month and a percentage of all money gifts and earnings, is another good way to grow perseverance. The blackberry-growing brothers took that next step and opened a savings account when their first profits came in. I think their wise grandpa may have had something to do with giving them a ride to the bank. After several years of growing and selling blackberries, these boys have saved enough money to finance a major part of their college educations.

- *Building a collection* of stamps, coins, rocks and minerals, or even baseball cards, over time is a painless perseverance-builder. Help your child organize the contents of the collection so it doesn't turn into a messy pile in a cabinet. Collectibles can be stored in shoe boxes, clear plastic bins, albums, notebooks, and even egg cartons.

- *Adopting an elderly person in a nursing home* or in the neighborhood if you don't have one in the family is another possibility. When you and your children faithfully visit a shut-in (even when you don't "feel" like it), they develop not only perseverance but a wonderful sense of compassion.

By the way, if you want to develop this character quality of perseverance, take steps to decrease your child's television watching. A steady diet of television viewing encourages quick fixes, easy thirty-minute answers to problems, and a very short attention span—just the opposite of what you're aiming for. Instead of TV, put out big 500- or 1000-piece puzzles and work on them as a family after dinner. Encourage art and crafts projects and games. Have your child involved in some chores that contribute to the family's well-being on a daily or weekly basis.

And when it's bedtime, and your child is all tuckered out from weeding the pumpkin patch or working on the rock collection, pull out some books and read to your child about people like Florence Nightingale, Amy Carmichael (missionary to India), Gladys Aylward (missionary to China), Joni Eareckson Tada, and many others, who persevered in spite of difficulties.

Read Bible stories about people who persevered, like Noah (whose building of the ark was not a short-term project!), Abraham, Daniel, and Paul. You can also find wonderful profiles of courageous people overcoming tragedy and failure in newspapers, in magazines like *Guideposts* and *Reader's Digest*. Clip and collect them in a "People Who Persevered" file. And don't forget to talk about why these people kept going and what we can learn from them.

Let me encourage you that if your child grows only 1 percent in perseverance each week, in a year you'll see a 50 percent growth. And if you keep it up, in two years, your child will be so persistent and determined you'll be amazed. And when that perseverance carries over to tackling school assignments, difficult tasks, and new challenges, your child will be prepared for a lifetime of learning.

LESSON OF THE DAY

Persevering people learn more and achieve more.

Raise a Reader

If you want your children to love to learn, ensure that they develop solid reading skills.

Did you know that if your children can read well, they will learn much more, and that after the third grade, success in *every subject* depends on reading ability?

That's why today's lesson is so important, for in it you'll discover some keys on how to raise a reader. Most parents have at least one child who is a "reluctant reader," a child who experiences difficulty learning to read or who just needs more practice and encouragement to become a fluent reader.

Academic learning, you see, starting with the 3 R's—reading, writing, and arithmetic—includes a great deal of listening and following directions, talking, writing, and especially *reading*. A child who has trouble with reading will usually struggle in other subjects as well. So developing strong reading skills in our kids should be a priority.

But in most homes parents aren't raising readers and writers but *watchers*—passive couch potatoes or video kids with hair-trigger attention spans. When young people spend most of their free time in TV and video pastimes, they simply are not prepared to operate successfully in the reading and writing demands of school.

HOW YOU CAN HELP

You may have thought that first grade was that magic time when kids learn how to read. But it actually begins much earlier. Your child's reading, like walking or talking, is a developmental process that begins the day of birth, and there is much you can do to help your young child become a fluent reader. Talking to your children while you point out the names of objects around you, singing to them, teaching nursery rhymes, answering the many "Why?" and "What's that?" questions, and reading while you snuggle them on your lap are all ways you're naturally laying a foundation for reading.

But reading *to* your children shouldn't stop when they learn to read in school. In fact, reading aloud at home is absolutely essential for a child to keep advancing in language skills. If a child isn't reading much at home, that child is likely to become part of the biggest educational problem facing America—a type of illiteracy in which people know how to read but *don't read*. That's why reading at home is vital.

Once your child learns to read, encourage independent reading. But continue reading aloud—the classics, a children's version of the Bible, and your own childhood favorites. What we find is that at the fourth grade level, kids' comprehension and vocabulary start declining—precisely the time when being read to is being left out of their lives, either because parents think the children ought to be able to read to themselves or because the parents are too busy.

Here are two read-aloud strategies that will encourage your child. Try one of them the next time you curl up on the couch:

- Read a story aloud and stop right before the end. Ask, "And now what do you think happened?" Encourage your child to make up the ending.
- When you're reading a chapter book (where the story line is divided into independent sections or chapters), stop at a crucial, suspenseful moment and say, "We'll find out what happens when we read tomorrow night." Let your child's wonder and excitement build in anticipation of your reading the next episode.

BUILD ON YOUR CHILD'S NATURAL INTERESTS

Let me share with you a secret that literacy tutors use when teaching someone to read. It works even with adults who never learned to read in school. The first step tutors take is to find out what a person is *most interested* in, what he wants to learn about and wishes he could read for himself. For one person it might be children's books, because he wants to be able to read to his children. For one young man, it might be a motorcycle manual; for another, the Bible.

Tap into your child's interests and you will light the fire of reading. I've seen this principle work over and over again. One day on an airplane I met William Jackson, one of America's top marine biologists. "I was a terrible reader all through elementary school," he told me, "until in the sixth grade when my aunt, who lived in Japan, heard I was interested in science. She sent me *The Omnibus of Science Fiction* for my birthday. Did that ever fire up my desire to read!"

The Omnibus of Science Fiction was a huge volume with sixty stories about space adventures, new life forms, and scientists' accidents that ignited Jackson's imagination and stirred his love of science. He read the book four times and then went on to devour westerns, mysteries, and spy novels—he was hooked on books! Later, Jackson pursued his love of science and now heads the National Marine Fisheries Service.

With Susan, the little girl I tutor every week in a Whiz Kids ministry for at-risk, inner-city children, I found the same positive effect by tapping into her interests. Susan, a fourth grader, was mainly interested in easier books and had some reading problems. But after introducing her to several different series, we happened upon the Molly series in the American Girl books, and the match lit the fire! Susan loves history, and each series about a different girl—Molly, Savannah, Abby—is set in a different period of American history, with an interesting background of that historical period in the back of each book.

We read *Changes for Molly,* and Susan couldn't wait to hear more about Molly, so I got *Molly's Christmas,* and then the summer Molly book, and then the next in the series. These books were harder than those that Susan was used to reading, but she was willing to plow through them because of her high interest level. The only way one's reading improves is by being challenged, by reading harder books. At Christmas I surprised Susan with another Molly book, which she read at home on her own. A thorough Molly fan, she said, "I wish I could write to the author."

I encouraged Susan to do just that, and she penned a letter to author Valerie Tripp. Within two weeks, Susan received a wonderful letter from the author with a fascinating brochure describing the inspiration from Valerie's own childhood for every one of the Molly books. What a thrill for Susan! The more she read, the better her reading skills became.

APPLYING THE HIGH-INTEREST PRINCIPLE TO READING

This is an easy lesson to apply. If you know what your children are most interested in knowing more about, get books and magazines on those subjects. If one is interested in topography, find books with pictures of volcanoes. If it's science fiction, there are numerous science fiction books for young readers. Libraries, bookstores, used book fairs and sales, garage sales—all are good resources to build your child's own personal library of high-interest materials.

Movies and documentary videos in your child's interest area can also motivate reading. Even reluctant readers get excited to read if they watch a movie, such as *Black Beauty*, before the book is assigned. After a group of students at our school watched the movies *Anne of Green Gables* and *Raise the Titanic*, all the books on those subjects quickly disappeared from the shelves of the school library.

When the school year is over and summer begins, don't let reading stop or many of the skills will be lost. Sign your children up for a summer reading program at a local library, which will help them set goals and will offer great incentives to read. When I took Susan to sign up for the Summer Reading Club, called "Be a Super Snooper Sleuth," she set a goal to read five books a week. She received a book bag, bookmark, and reading log. For reaching her summer goal, she'll receive a wonderful gold medal on a red Olympic-style ribbon and tickets to a children's theater production and a professional baseball game.

If your child's reading is not progressing or if it's below grade level, find a qualified person to evaluate your child's reading skills. Find out what the problem is. Get help and keep reading aloud to your child at home, regularly. Don't accept a "reading disabled" label from your child's school. Every child can learn to read, because learn-to-read programs have been developed for almost every type of learning style and disability.[1] One-on-one tutoring also can make a tremendous difference. Model the interest and skills you want to instill in your child, enjoy reading aloud together at home, and continue to encourage your child to read. You'll be helping one of the most important parts of the learning process—raising a lifelong reader!

LESSON OF THE DAY

Boost your children's reading skills by tapping into their interests and by reading aloud at home.

Help Your Child Become a Lively Thinker

Thinking is perhaps the most important subject of all, and it begins at home.

If you and I have the same amount of money, how much must I give you so that you'll have $10 more than I do? Think about it! If you're like most adults of normal intelligence, you were stumped or gave the wrong answer. It's five dollars.[1] In groups of adults who were given this and other challenging questions to consider, only four out of ten people could solve it.

Today's kids tend to be even weaker in the thinking and problem-solving department than adults. Have you ever looked at how your child answered a test question or math problem and said, "You're just not thinking!"? Many students think only vertically—they just keep thinking more and more but in the same direction. Lateral thinkers try one vein of thinking and then try looking at the problem from a whole different angle. If that doesn't work, they start over in another place.

Don't despair. Regardless of your child's present thinking skills, the ability to think and solve problems effectively can be learned, and that's what our focus is for today's lesson. The best place to learn thinking skills is at home, with you as the "Thinking Professor," using everyday activities and routines.

Just as children's hair colors, skin tones, and personalities are unique, so are their brains. If one of the mind-stretchers below doesn't click with your child, try a different one (or pose it six months from now; youthful brains are growing all the time and they can understand or easily solve something that stumped them only a few months earlier). Make lively thinking a part of your family's lifestyle rather than a rare occurrence. Not only will you enjoy it but your children will achieve more in every area.

PUT ON YOUR THINKING CAP

All the talking you do with your child (see Day 4) is valuable for building conversation skills, vocabulary, and thinking abilities. All the language a child hears in the early years lays circuitry in the mind that will be there for the rest of the child's life. Those mental structures are the "tracks" your child's thinking, speaking, and learning will run on, so maximize them. Speak with a rich, colorful vocabulary and in complex, rather than just simple, sentences. Use past, present, and future tenses; talk about cause and effect ("If this happens, then . . .").

In addition, all you learned on Day 6 about exposing your child to music connects here. Even fun music activities—like listening to classical music, playing "Clap a Rhythm" (clap a rhythm out and then have your child repeat it to you), or starting a sequence of notes (like the first line of a song) and then having your child complete it—are brain stretchers that enhance kids' thinking abilities.

Try the following thinking activities based on questioning that moves from the simplest level to more complex, critical thinking. You can adapt these to anything your child is studying or learning about:

1. *Knowing Basic Information:* Does your child know the basic facts? Can your child remember or list the material learned, like the addition facts or vocabulary words? Or in a story, how did the main character get out of prison?

2. *Comprehending and Interpreting:* Can your child see the connection between facts or know the meaning of the material? Can your child explain or summarize the material? (Have your child retell a story orally after reading it. Or look at a magazine picture and ask, "Can you tell me what's happening and what might happen next?" Or have your child teach you math concepts using a blackboard.)

3. *Applying:* Can your child use the material learned and skills acquired on one problem to solve a similar problem? (Like writing and performing a puppet script based on a story just read, writing a different but plausible ending for a story, writing a word problem that uses math facts being studied.)

4. *Analyzing:* Can your child break the material into its parts and see the relationship between them? (After reading a simple news story from a local newspaper, make a grid and break down the information into *who, what, where, when, and why important*). You also can encourage analytical thinking by giving your children reasons for what you do and encourage them to provide reasons for what they do. Talk about *why* things happen as you analyze world events.

5. *Synthesizing:* Can a child go beyond the learned material to combine, create, or put together something new? (Take the same news story and rewrite it from an entirely different point of view or focus.) *How* questions encourage synthesizing, such as, "How would our country have been different if the British had won the Revolutionary War?"

77

6. *Evaluating:* Can your children interpret, critique, or judge new material based on evidence they have learned? (Talk about and evaluate a TV program after you have watched it with your children. Writing a review of a movie in which they advise someone why the movie is worthwhile to see or evaluating a chapter on algebraic formulas in a math book also builds thinking skills.)

Remember, the more interesting and complex the questions are, the more children are challenged to think analytically and creatively.

MIND-STRETCHING PROBLEMS

Use opportunities in real, everyday living to give your children problem-solving practice. Let them help figure out how far apart to space vegetable and flower seedlings in your garden. When you're going on a family trip, let your kids help plan and budget the vacation money. They also can help the driver navigate using maps while enroute to your destination.

Provide measuring tools and give problems to solve. A ruler, a map and compass, an egg timer, balance scales, and thermometers are a good start. Then pose a question like: How much carpet will it take to recarpet the living room? How long will it take us to get to Uncle John's at a speed of sixty miles per hour? When you have an apparent problem in the household, like how to keep the dog from tearing up the newly planted shrubs in the backyard, bring your children into the discussion and search for solutions together. You may be surprised at the creative ideas they come up with!

Brainstorming is excellent practice for thinking skills and helps children see different options instead of getting snagged by having only one way to look at a problem. Study an object, such as a plastic foam meat tray (the kind that meat comes in at the grocery store), and figure out how many different uses there could be for it. Also try duct tape, a toothpick, and a paper clip. This is not only great for encouraging divergent, creative thinking, it's also a lot of fun to do together or as teams, jotting down all the possible uses and then comparing how many each team (or person) came up with.

Play games that require logical reasoning and strategy, such as chess or Battleship. In addition, when your kids ask for new privileges, have them make a list of the pros and cons for you to consider.

Today, I encourage you to apply one of the questions in the "Put On Your Thinking Cap" section to whatever your child is assigned for homework or is interested in. When children begin to see themselves as thinkers and have several opportunities to problem solve, think creatively, and discuss important issues at home, their mental development will be enhanced, and they'll enjoy learning more in every subject.

LESSON OF THE DAY

Good thinkers are good learners, and parents can have a terrific impact on their children's developing thinking skills.

Raise a Writer

Becoming a better writer will sharpen your child's learning skills and fuel achievement.

A great way to gear your children for learning is to help them become better writers.

Writing demands clarity of thought and challenges us to come up with the right word to express our thoughts and ideas. Good writers become good thinkers and more motivated learners. They also earn higher grades in the myriad of writing assignments that students must do—from third grade book reports to essay questions on tests and chemistry lab reports in high school.

Helping your child become a better writer is not as difficult as it may sound. Regardless of how you did in writing assignments when you were in school, you can give your child writing practice at home without resorting to workbooks or formal lessons. From years of teaching children and teens to write reports, research papers, stories, and poems, I've found that kids who write at home do much better in any writing tasks they are given at school.

And that doesn't mean they have to write lengthy essays to hone their skills. Writing notes to each other on a regular basis and posting them on a central family bulletin board gives writing practice and, at the same time serves as reminders for chores (instead of nagging), gives encouragement ("I'm cheering for you on your spelling test today! Love, Dad"), and enhances a busy family's communication. Or have your child make a Family Mailbox out of a shoe box, markers, and other craft materials—it makes a great place to exchange notes and have confidential chats with siblings and parents.

Writing also becomes more meaningful when it's used to record memorable events. You can set out a blank notebook for family writing and start a "family journal." Anyone can write (even younger pre-readers can dictate their rendition of "Our Trip to the Zoo" while parent or older sibling puts pen to paper), and if Mom and Dad both write regularly and encourage the children to participate, the family journal can become a real treasure. Entries can include reflections on graduation or other ceremonies, family field trips and outings, visits from relatives or special people, and descriptions of storms and unusual occurrences.

LETTER WRITING

Letters can be personal, expressive, and creative and are easy to write with a little instruction. For a child, there's nothing better than getting your very own letter in the mailbox from someone special. It doesn't matter whether it's via "snail mail" (through the U.S. Postal Service) or corresponding over interstate and country-to-country lines by using electronic mail, also called "e-mail." A child who has a regular pen pal or someone who will write and respond quickly can get a lively correspondence going that is a great boost to writing skills. The pen pal can be a favorite grandparent or a best friend who moved away or a camp buddy.

When I was in early elementary school, my uncle in Alaska and I wrote letters and sent photos, cartoons, and other fun stuff. This provided an essential element every young writer needs: an audience to write for. When the only feedback kids get on the papers they write is the red marks from their teacher's pen, they get discouraged instead of encouraged to write. What my uncle provided was positive feedback on a regular basis. He answered my questions about Eskimos and igloos (I'd only seen pictures of them in an encyclopedia) and asked me questions about my siblings and what we were doing at school and in our family.

Letter writing is excellent practice for other kinds of writing. Did you know that Alex Haley, award-winning author of *Roots* and other books and screenplays, honed his talent for writing while aboard Coast Guard ships during his years of duty? He began writing love letters for other sailors to send home to girlfriends and wives, and his writing career eventually took off.

Yes, I know it's easier to pick up a phone and call someone instead of writing a letter, but if you can resurrect the art of letter writing in your family, your child will reap terrific benefits.

LETTERS FOR FUN AND FREE STUFF

There's a kind of letter I've found kids like to write that will fuel their interest in correspondence: a letter asking for free stuff. When our children were young, I found there are hundreds of things they can send for—most for free or under $1. We discovered stickers, hobby materials, NASA space stuff, sports cards, "Neon Frog Paper," and even model rockets—all available by sending a postcard or letter. Now this got them to writing!

You can find addresses for free stuff—how-to craft guides, Power Ranger stickers, games and such—by looking in the various books at a local public library or bookstore, like *Free Stuff for Kids* (Meadowbrook Press) or *Freebies for Kids* (Contemporary Books). Provide paper or postcards, envelopes, pen, and a small book of stamps, and then make sure your child follows the directions for each object or material requested. Soon you'll find your child checking the mailbox almost every day to see if the latest "free stuff" has arrived.

WRITE TO YOUR KIDS

Write to your older kids and teens, letting them know you love and appreciate them or that you're proud of them. Children are sometimes embarrassed to hear "lovey stuff" spoken out loud, but they need the love and affirmation. When you put your feelings into letters to your kids, it becomes one of their cherished possessions.

WRITING IN REAL-WORLD SITUATIONS

Let your child see you writing a letter to the editor of your local newspaper or favorite magazine, writing to the cable company about a disputed bill, or penning a thank-you note to a friend. If your children see you valuing writing and doing your own as part of your everyday life, chances are they will learn to value writing, too. (There's that powerful "role-modeling" principle again. It works so well with whatever we want to impart to our children because they imitate our actions much more than our words!)

One fine family tradition to start is this: With every Christmas stocking, include a small box of thank-you notes (maybe even with each child's name or initial stamped colorfully on the

Children need models so they can see what a certain form of writing is supposed to look like. Tack up on the bulletin board a standard letter format that includes the following elements:

Date

Name _____

Address _____

City, State, Zip _____

Dear Grandma,

Body of letter _____

_____

_____

_____

_____

_____

Love,

Jennifer

top). Then when it's time to dismantle the tree and pack away the decorations, serve some cookies while everyone sits around the dining table and writes thank-you notes for the thoughtful gifts from grandparents and friends.

If you have a computer, your kids can create their own banners that say "Happy Birthday" or "Welcome Home," party invitations, and even door signs ("Brothers, keep out, just for today"). They can use computer graphics to add creative borders and other artwork to their letters and invitations.

As your family becomes "a writing family" and your children have natural opportunities to practice writing at home, they'll become more effective and skilled writers. They'll find they can use writing to build friendships, even across the miles. They'll become more self-motivated about doing homework, because much of it involves writing down information. They'll be able to use writing as an effective way to learn material—taking better class notes and organizing and remembering important ideas while studying for tests. Good writers are more successful in every subject at school, especially as they advance from elementary school to middle school, high school, and college.

Improved writing comes through numerous meaningful writing experiences. Have your child try one of these letter-writing ideas this week, for fun, free stuff, or friendship!

LESSON OF THE DAY

When children are encouraged to write regularly at home and share their writing with interested parents and friends, they become better writers—and learners!

Help Your Child Develop a Sharper Memory

Building memorization skills helps children become better learners and achieve more.

Although creative thinking and problem solving are very important, so is learning to memorize information. In much of progressive education in schools today, we've thrown the baby out with the bath water—favoring projects and critical thinking and cooperative groups over rote learning.

Let me explain. In all the efforts to teach the concepts of math—the "whys" and "hows"—many kids haven't been taught the "whats," which makes it hard for them to *use* the information. When students are trying to figure gas mileage or distance or mortgage interest, they need to know what 8 x 9 equals. If they memorize the multiplication tables, then long division, fractions, and algebra go much more smoothly. Knowing grammar and spelling rules, like "*i* before *e* except after *c*," aids writing skills, just as knowing the names of the

Great Lakes, the states, and capitals of the United States is essential to having a grasp of geography.

There are things you can do to help your child remember this and other information. Today's lesson focuses on some easy exercises you can teach your children that not only will sharpen their memory skills but also will be useful whenever they have to learn important information in a school subject.

MAKING MEMORIZATION WORK

A good memory isn't something static or fixed—something you have or don't have. With mental exercise, anyone's memory can get better. What matters is what you do to remember information. Memorizing information doesn't have to be boring; in fact, it can be fun. Here are some enjoyable memory techniques and games to teach your child:

- *Make Up a Memory Song:* Do you remember the tune that for decades has helped kids learn their ABCs? Your child can make up a song to learn the fifty states, the books of the Bible, the presidents of the United States, dates in history, or even long lists of information. Already created songs are great (like the "Alphabet Song"), but when children participate in making up the song, they tend to remember it much better.

  You can also use a familiar melody and put new words to it that incorporate the facts to be memorized. For example, to help your child remember the five vowels, sing "Old MacDonald's Farm" like this: "Old MacDonald had a farm—*A, E, I, O, U.*" Or compose a song with an entirely new melody.

  Add gestures or hand movements to a song while learning information and they will help cue memory and aid recall, especially for children who are "Movers." (See Day 3, "Teach Your Child to Study Smarter.")

- *Organize the Information:* Whatever your child needs to learn, show how to organize it in a logical sequence. For example, if your child is trying to memorize a list of fruits to get at the store (watermelons, mangos, avocados, apples, bananas, and cantaloupes), use the first letter of each fruit to form a single word: W-A-M for watermelon, avocado, and mango, and C-A-B for cantaloupes, apples, and bananas.

   For remembering the names of the Great Lakes, use H-O-M-E-S for Huron, Ontario, Michigan, Erie, Superior. This kind of memory booster (called an acrostic or acronym) can help your child learn the names of the planets, metric measurements, or even the colors of the spectrum.

- *Sentence Chain:* Another effective memory aid is a sentence chain. The first letter of each word in a sentence stands for a key word or idea. One chain I taught my geography students when they needed to memorize the seven continents of the world is: "Aunt Alice ate apples nearly every Saturday," which stands for Africa, Asia, Australia, Antarctica, North America, Europe, and South America. Another is "Never Eat Sour Weiners" to help them remember the directions north, east, south, west. If your children make up the sentence chain or acrostic, they'll remember it better.

Memory aids like these use sound, repetition, humor, creativity, and sometimes a little silliness. They enable students to learn and memorize much more information than they could otherwise. You probably created some of these yourself when you were in school studying for a big test. If so, share some of your own memory aids with your child.

BECOME THE TEACHER!

Whenever I teach in a classroom, whether for a group of young authors, college students, or at a writer's conference, I'm reminded of how much I—the teacher—get to learn. It's amazing! Think about the last time you taught a Bible study, a workshop at your company, or a Sunday school class. Who learned and remembered the most?

In fact, research shows that students who teach information to other people retain *90 percent* of the material.[1] Your child can use a white chalkless board and markers to review a section of information being studied, then teach it to you, to sisters and brothers, or to a study partner.

Dr. Mike Jones used this method to go from straight F's to straight A's in college. He was a poor student throughout high school and failed the first two semesters of college. Then he found that if he took his notes, picked a bite-size portion of the information, and reviewed it until he could lay his notes down and explain it out loud, in his own words as if there were a class there, he remembered the material much better and made a higher grade.

By actively "teaching" this way, Mike found his comprehension and memory of the material improved dramatically. He began earning A's in every course, achieving his first 4.0 grade point average that semester. Mike kept his 4.0 throughout the rest of his college years, went on to earn a doctorate, and has taught the method to hundreds of people in business, colleges, schools, and even home schools. He tells the whole story in his book *The Overnight Student*.[2] Suggest this study method the next time there's a test or anything to learn and watch your child's grades and confidence go up.

EXERCISING VISUAL MEMORY

Some of the best test takers and learners I know utilize their visual memories to master information. Do you remember a classmate who would gaze briefly at the spelling list and in no time recite every word, spelled correctly? This student probably had a sharp visual memory that takes a quick "snapshot" of the words in her mind's eye. When it's time to write them on a test, these "snapshots" can easily be retrieved to show the correctly spelled words on that mental screen.

Don't be discouraged if your child isn't this kind of learner. Even kids who don't naturally utilize their visual memories in school can learn to do so. Here's a good way, using "Funny Connections": Your child can make somewhat crazy associations to memorize two items that go together, such as books and authors, people and places, or states and capitals. For example, to remember that the capital of New Hampshire is Concord, suggest picturing the ham in *Ham*pshire covered with Concord grape juice. Or to remember the meaning of Roman numerals, try: D = 500 (In*dy* 500), or C = 100 (a century is 100 years), or M = 1000 (the Milky Way has thousands of stars).

To improve visual memory, have your child play games like "Concentration." To play, you need a pack of cards. Deal out every card in the deck face down on the table. Each player takes a turn, turning over two cards at a time, trying to find matches or pairs of cards. If a player's two cards match, that player gets another turn until the two cards turned over don't match. Then the play passes to the next player. Continue until all cards are in matches.

Or let your child play the "Memory Game": Place five to ten objects on a cookie sheet or tray one at a time, (toy car, ball-point pen, paper clip, action figure, and dollar bill, for example). Have your children look at the objects intently for forty-five to sixty seconds. Then remove the tray and have them close their eyes and see if they can "see" and name the objects. Then ask: Can you name them in the order they appeared on the tray? Can you name them in reverse? As they are successful, add objects to the tray to increase the challenge.

Play one of the games or activities from today's lesson and watch your child discover how much fun exercising the memory can be! Then, the next time there's a test, encourage your child to use one of these techniques to better memorize information. After the material is committed to memory, review it or give your child an opportunity to use it occasionally.

LESSON OF THE DAY

Building memorization skills helps children to become better learners and to achieve much more.

Teach Responsibility

Children who develop the quality of responsibility through chores and tasks at home learn more and do better in school.

Did you know that by the time your children are ready to receive their "wings" when they graduate from high school and leave home, they will have spent 32,234 hours under your supervision, training, and guidance? Compare that to the mere 2,100 hours of classroom and study time it takes to earn a bachelor's degree in college. You have *sixteen times more* teaching and training hours with your child than all the time with professors and dorm time combined in an entire university education.[1] Wow, that's a lot of time!

Sure, some of that time is spent eating and reading, practicing sports, and playing in the backyard or neighborhood, which are all wonderful uses of time—but some of the best uses of that time are the teachable moments in which your child learns *responsibility*. It's one of the greatest life skills your child can ever learn. If we give our kids too much, do everything for them, and expect little in return, we fail to instill in them a sense of family teamwork, security, and responsibility.

One of the main ways to teach responsibility at home is through doing regular chores. What does such responsibility have to do with learning? Kids who have chores at home and develop a sense of responsibility tend to be much better students who write assignments down, complete them, learn more, and make higher grades. They have more confidence and more coping skills. And if they become responsible, your children will not only be more successful in school but later, in jobs, in their careers, and even in their own marriages and families.

The events and daily goings-on of family life offer a myriad of opportunities to help children grow in responsibility. Today we're going to look at how.

LIFE'S LITTLE LESSONS

I'm all for kids having a fun childhood with plenty of time for play, friendship, and family outings. I don't advocate having children assume adult responsibilities too early or become the family maid. But when a child has regular chores on which the family's well-being depends, a wonderful sense of responsibility and self-worth grows. In addition, that child tends to develop a sense of initiative, which means figuring out what needs to be done and not having to be told everything. And it happens step by little step.

Developing a sense of responsibility starts as early as the preschool years, as you encourage your three-year-old to help you in little ways in the kitchen and teach him to do simple household chores. Little kids feel big when they get to "help mommy cook" or help daddy pick up leaves in the yard or "mow" the grass beside him with a Fisher-Price plastic mower.

One of the secrets of building a sense of responsibility is recognizing the age-appropriate ways children can help around the house. Otherwise, if we give them too heavy a load of daily chores, they feel overwhelmed or eventually become resentful. A two-year-old, for example, could pick up his toys and put them in colorful plastic bins, pick up clothes and put them in drawers that have picture labels of "Socks and Batman underwear," "Jeans," "T-shirts." He could also begin to make his bed (with help from Mom). But washing the dishes and taking out the garbage every day would not fit a two-year-old's abilities and skills.

Young children can feed the dog, make beds, pick up teddy bears and playthings, and do other simple chores. Six-year-olds can take their dishes to the kitchen, put dirty clothes in the hamper, and make their beds. Older children can set the dinner table, empty wastebaskets, load and unload dishes in the dishwasher—and eventually help with yard work.

An experience a father I know had with his son illustrates how well we can shave down tasks to the right child-size. One day Flip's little boy Matthew was helping him load tree limbs that Flip had cut down with a chain saw. Dad sliced up the limbs of the big oak tree, but the pieces were too heavy for Matthew to carry. So he sliced them again with the chain saw, but the pieces were still too heavy.

Finally, Flip cut the wood into even smaller pieces. Matt could pick them up and he proudly carried load after load to the truck. Not only did he learn that his dad was determined to work with him, Matt saw that his dad cared more about him than about getting the job done fast.

Whenever possible, break jobs into small bites or steps so they are manageable for your child. And be patient—it takes a young child longer to do a task than it takes an adult. Then when the job's done, affirm your child's efforts by showing how pleased you are: "You worked so hard! I appreciate what a willing spirit you had." Avoid re-doing the work your children have done or you'll discourage their initiative.

WORKING AT HOME

I admit that not every child is going to be as cooperative as Matthew. With some kids we have to be creative about devising ways to get them to do their share of housework. Some parents I know have used charts successfully. They make a chart or calendar for each child and post it on their bedroom doors or family bulletin board, writing down the chores that each child is to do. Then when the job is done, the child gets to put a sticker in that space and at the end of the week, if a certain percentage of chores are completed, Mom or Dad gives a reward.

Charts often work well in fostering follow-through, especially for young children learning basic skills like brushing teeth, making a bed, and picking up toys. Charts are useful in the summer when kids may tend to "veg out" in front of the television (I hope yours don't. If so, review Days 4 and 10). Sometimes charts or daily "To Do" lists are effective with older children when they get sloppy and inconsistent with their chores.

Many kids love crossing off each item on their daily chart; it gives them a sense of accomplishment. Even pre-readers can read and follow instructions on a daily chart when pictures are used to indicate the tasks (Teeth: Draw or cut out a picture of a toothbrush from a magazine; Pick Up Toys: Picture of ball and toy cars).

THE FAMILY TEAM

If a chart works well to help your children remember to get their chores done, that's great. I have to admit that I'm a dropout where charts are concerned. What worked better for us over the long haul was getting the family together as a team to tackle household chores. We often picked a Saturday morning. I wrote out a list on a big sheet of paper of all the jobs that needed to be done. On a typical Saturday our "To Do" list might include: dust furniture, vacuum carpets, gather all garbage and take out, clean bathroom sinks and toilets (not the most popular job!), polish mirrors with Windex.

On the right-hand side of the page beside each task was an approximation of how long it would take to complete, and in the left margin, a blank line—where we would fill in our names as we chose our chores. Then we turned on the music and got to work. In two hours or less, the work was done and we'd all celebrate by going out for pizza or a bike ride. In working together, a real sense of teamwork and cooperation developed among us and at the same time the kids were learning some valuable life skills. Justin, Chris, and Alison liked the fact that chores could change from week to week and that they had some choice of which jobs to tackle. However, don't think we didn't make a bed or wash a dish until Saturday—those were everyday duties each person was responsible for.

When kids say, "I can't do that," they may mean, "I don't know how!" Use a patient, step-by-step approach to demonstrate a new task. Allow practice until your child is ready to move on. Demonstrate the right products to use and the best method to do the task, and don't expect perfection. Since some children like to work more independently and others want a show-and-tell approach—working with parents until they feel competent doing the chore—allow for different working styles.

However, I find that most children need some kind of list. We shouldn't tell them five tasks to accomplish in one hour and expect them to remember and complete them. A few children with terrific auditory memories may be able to remember a sequence of verbal instructions and tasks to do on their own, but the majority (especially young children and many boys) would get sidetracked after the second or third chore. Do what works best with your child's way of learning and remembering things.

Then, don't forget to give plenty of positive feedback, even if the job isn't done perfectly. Remember, focus on that donut—the progress, the effort your child put in—and you'll build your child's motivation for helping and doing chores at home, and thus, your child's sense of responsibility.

Avoid comparing one sibling's work or performance on a job with another sibling's. Give each one little snapshots of their own abilities and character qualities with comments such as, "You really know how to rearrange things and turn a mess into a lovely place" when your son cleans and reorganizes his room, or "The way you helped me get the table set when company was coming over tonight was a lifesaver. Thanks for cooperating!" or "You've remembered to feed the dog every day this week. That's really *being responsible!*"

Natural consequences are always a boost when building responsibility. For example, when trying to help your children accept responsibility for homework, don't pick up the burden and do assignments for them if they fall down on the job. Let them experience the consequences and make a lower grade.

If your children leave clothes, toys, and other personal possessions lying around on the floor of the living room or common family areas, use the "Saturday Box" consequence. It's the best way I've found to nudge children to pick up their belongings without constant nagging. When you find kids' stuff on the floor, gather them in a "Saturday Box" where they are put up and unattainable until the next weekend. Most kids quickly learn to put things away where they belong when a logical consequence such as this is used.

LESSON OF THE DAY

Children who develop the quality of responsibility through chores and tasks at home learn more and do better in school.

Handling Homework

Finding the balance between your child's part and your part.

- The teacher says, "Your daughter sure works at her own pace!" She really might be saying, "Susie's turned in all of her work late."
- You get so fed up with your child's piles of homework that you tell the teacher, "You certainly focus on high achievement in your class, don't you?" You really want to say, "Don't you think five hours of homework a night is a bit too much?"

In many families, homework hassles abound. Since studies show that children who regularly complete homework assignments learn and achieve much more,[1] we know it's important. Yet struggling with homework is the number one problem that both parents and teachers complain about.

With good intentions, parents sometimes take over and do the work for their kids, depriving them of any sense of initiative or ownership. What is healthy involvement with homework and what is interference? Let's spend today finding the balance between your part and your child's part and in the process discover some creative solutions that will maximize learning.

GET ORGANIZED!

The first step is to help your child get organized. Some kids are so orderly they color code their hangers and have equidistant space between each item in their closet; school organization is usually a breeze for these students. Or maybe your child is like one of my mine. When you look in her notebook or locker, there are numerous papers crumpled inside, along with Barbie stickers, candy wrappers, and last week's math assignment that she forgot to turn in.

Discovering some organizational skills that work for your child might be just the key, because throughout twenty-five years of teaching and working with kids, I've found that disorganization is a leading cause of failure, discouragement, and a lack of motivation. It's hard to learn anything when you can't even find your book or remember the assignments you're supposed to do!

While some children are natural organizers, the majority need help keeping assignments, books, and papers straight (especially those kids with any kind of learning problem). The following organizers will go a long way toward making learning a rewarding experience:

- Organize a quiet space for your child to work in. If she insists she needs music playing, I suggest classical music because it enhances brain function rather than interferes with it. Include a good lamp, a desk, bookshelves, dictionary, pencils and pens, and a stand-up file with file folders labeled "Tests" and "Homework" or whatever suits the courses being studied. In addition, a typewriter or computer is helpful if one is available. Add a couple of brightly colored storage boxes: one for school papers and the other for supplies.

- Supplies that will aid learning include: notebook paper, stapler or paper clips, a pack of 3 x 5 index cards for making study cards in any subject, a tape recorder and blank tapes, a kitchen timer to mark study time and breaks, and a pad to write down a checklist of tasks for each study session and to cross them off as completed. A few sheets of large poster board are worth having on hand to save you last-minute trips to the store when a project is due.

- Some kind of assignment notebook or calendar is a *must* for students to write down assignments. My favorite, especially through the middle-school years, is a weekly assignment calendar that you can make with a ruler and blank typing paper, creating blocks for each subject and day of the week. Let your child decorate the border and then photocopy a bunch of these calendars. Every Monday morning your child replaces last week's calendar with a fresh calendar. Have her staple it to the front of her notebook so she can take it to class each day and record the assignments. If she consistently forgets to write down the tasks in a subject block, suggest to the teacher that he jog your child's memory by initialing the sheet each day until it becomes a habit.

SAME TIME, SAME PLACE

Remember the concept behind this book and the others in the *21 DAY* series? If you do something for twenty-one consecutive days, it becomes a habit. Well, that's talking about an adult. For school-age children, it takes about four to six days to formulate a habit pattern because their brains are younger and faster than ours![2] If you want your children to develop a habit of daily study, have them study in the same place at approximately the same time each day. After about six days, they won't be debating "Should I do my homework, or not?" They'll just come in and get to work.

Why? "Our minds become accustomed to *daily patterns*," says Dr. Wanda Draper, associate professor of psychiatry at the University of Oklahoma College of Medicine. For example, you don't put extensive decision making into whether to brush your teeth each morning and night. You probably do it out of habit (or else your mate or friends and coworkers will find your breath a little disagreeable!).

In the same way, you don't want your kids deliberating about whether to do their homework—they should do it naturally. And if you start them in a positive pattern of studying at the same time and place, especially at the first of the school year, they'll become consistent, more focused, and will actually learn more. Study may even become second nature, like brushing teeth. And if you're still having to remind your children to brush their teeth—take heart! When the phone starts ringing for dates, you'll be out of a job. In fact, they'll probably ask you to get mouthwash, too.

If this "routine" and pattern stuff sounds a little too structured, read what learning specialist Faith Clark, Ph.D., says: "Structure and ritual, including regular meal and bedtimes, the bedtime story and other daily traditions, form the foundation for learning. . . . A home without ritual is a home with a high prospect of homework problems."[3] These routines at home provide the structure kids need to stay on track throughout the school year and to focus and concentrate on learning.

What about the question of *when* and *how long* the study time should be? For most children, having a snack after school and some time to unwind and play before sitting down to do home-work works well. But if a child's "peak" time of mental alertness is early morning, that might be the best time to study. In any case, decide with your child on a time and post it as a reminder. And be aware that kids in fifth grade or younger can normally study fifteen minutes at a time, take a five-minute break, and then study for another fifteen minutes, while older students can easily study thirty minutes at a time with five-minute breaks. Setting a kitchen timer really helps focus them for those periods of time.

AVOID INTERFERENCE

Just as the athlete is the one who must get down on the field or court and do the actual playing while the coach stands on the sideline, encouraging and instructing, homework is your child's responsibility—and your part is to encourage learning and help your child establish good homework habits. With that in mind, avoid doing your child's homework yourself, even when the hour is late, your child needs to get to bed, and you could do it faster. That just encourages dependency and help-lessness (as well as dishonesty) in your child.

Show genuine interest in what your child is studying and doing at school. Instead of asking, "Do you have any homework today?" (to which most kids give the classic answer, "No, I don't think so," when they really have a book report due in two weeks and twenty vocabulary words to learn by Friday's test), ask, "What kind of math assignment are you going to tackle today?" or "Which sub-ject are you planning on starting first, reading or math?"

Help your child break big tasks into small, manageable chunks and then make each "chunk" a goal for one study ses-sion. For example, if a sixteen-page chapter is assigned on Mon-day for reading by Friday, the goal could be four pages a day.

If you help your children get organized and reward them with encouraging words and hugs for homework that's done well, you'll find your children's learning will increase and the homework hassles will diminish.

LESSON OF THE DAY

Help your child get organized for homework. Find the balance between encouragement and interference.

See That Your Child Succeeds at Something

Look for ways to encourage and develop your child's talents.

Jake and Luke Thoene, sons of award-winning authors Bodie and Brock Thoene, have published the eighth novel in their successful youth series "The Baker Street Mysteries"—a huge accomplishment for guys in their twenties. But Jake, the oldest, hasn't always had such success. Regularly ridiculed by teachers or other students, Jake struggled with dyslexia (as did his mom) and had many problems in school. In fact, Jake and Bodie both sport T-shirts that read: "Bad Spellers of the World, Untie!"

For Jake, the turnaround came when he participated in a school yearbook project in junior high and found he could succeed at something. "I was layout editor," says Jake. "I learned how to crop photos and sell advertisements to raise the money to publish the yearbook. That experience is probably the most significant academic accomplishment I had up to that point in my life. My confidence rose 1000%."[1]

In spite of learning difficulties or weaknesses, every person wants desperately to be valued, appreciated, and respected. The need to achieve in some area is just as much of a basic human need as is a sense of belonging and security. Finding *something* you can be competent or successful in is what develops self-confidence. Kids don't just develop high self-esteem because they're told, "You're great" or "You're wonderful"; they develop it from being able to *do* something well that they consider worthwhile.

I've found that for most of us parents, we can't get by with wishing the school or other adults will discover and develop our children's gifts. It's nice if they do, but we shouldn't hold our breath or leave it to them. Generally, only the students who are math-smart and/or language-smart—and thus make high test scores and grades—find success in traditional school situations. Many of the rest of the kids grow up feeling dumb or incompetent because their strengths aren't as readily recognized or rewarded.

Yet we know from over fifty years of research that report cards and IQ tests don't tell the whole story of a child's potential. The standardized kind of paper-and-pencil testing doesn't reveal one child's perfect pitch and musical ability, another's terrific people skills or artistic talent. But let me encourage you: Einstein's genius or Churchill's leadership skills weren't revealed by school situations either. Neither were the incredible technical skill, dexterity, and determination that enabled Dr. Fred Epstein, one of the world's top neurosurgeons, to operate on and remove lethal tumors from the tiny brain stems of children. In fact, Epstein was once a poor student and was rejected by four medical schools.

Questions like these are better determiners of talent:

- Has your child always been good with words and at making up imaginative stories?
- Does your child have special physical fluidity and coordination that show up on the athletic field or in dance?
- Has your child been able to remember and repeat tunes since he was very young?

- Is your child often the leader of the group, able to organize other kids into action—whether it's a Scout fund-raising project or building a neighborhood tree fort?

These abilities may be keys to your children's potential. According to Dr. Howard Gardner, author of *Frames of Mind: The Theory of Multiple Intelligence*, parent observation is the very best indicator of a child's intelligence and talent.[2] And if we understand and appreciate these gifts and know how to encourage them, our children develop a positive sense of self-worth, are happier, and tend to find purpose and direction for their lives. They also develop momentum in their learning and classroom experiences.

DIFFERENT SMARTS

What are some of these different talents that you might want to look for in your child? One is spatial intelligence—this is a creative person who visualizes naturally and loves to draw or design things. Like Anne Geddes, a world-famous photographer who's taken pictures of babies as angels, ladybugs, little birds, and even carrots. You've probably seen calendars, posters, and greeting cards with her baby photos on them.

"Whenever I see an image of something, in my mind, I see a baby in it," says Geddes.[3] That's a spatially smart person, all right. Spatially intelligent people also become architects and artists, sculptors, or art teachers.

Then there are body-smart kids with physical or athletic talent. While other babies were playing with rattles, little Tiger Woods was playing with a tiny golf club. When he was six, he could beat half the people who played at his dad's golf course. Eventually he became the youngest person to ever win the Master's Tournament. Tiger's tremendous coordination, dexterity, and physical fluidity contribute to his success. Actors, dancers, mechanics, and even neurosurgeons also have this kind of gift.

OPEN DOORS

David M. is another talented young man, but you couldn't tell it by his success in the educational system. Severe ear infections in infancy left David with impaired hearing discrimination, which caused him major struggles in school (diagnostic testing revealed that he could clearly distinguish about 5 percent of what the teacher was saying in class). His mother, Elaine, gave him a lot of additional tutoring through his elementary and middle school years, but when he entered ninth grade, no matter how many hours he studied, he just couldn't keep up with the work.

Elaine began to worry that David wouldn't have the academic skills he needed to prepare for a career or compete in the job market. She wondered if he would even be able to graduate from high school. Her concerns led her to join a Mom's In Touch group, to pray with other mothers for the teachers and kids. As she prayed for David, she began to realize that God had an exciting plan for her son and that God had all the power and connections to bring his plan to fruition. David began taking courses he was really interested in instead of just the college-bound courses. He still had a hard time with some of the book work, but his faith and hope were growing.

One of the areas he developed an interest in was computers, and through classes and part-time jobs his talent blossomed. Students and teachers came to him with questions, and he discovered that he also had a knack for helping people.

When he graduated successfully, David decided to enter a local junior college. He registered for some computer-animation classes. He did well and joined a special-project team to produce a college catalog on CD-ROM. The project won an award.

The next year, David was asked to lead the CD-ROM project, to teach two college seminars in a new computer animation language, and to tutor students. A Christian university saw his CD-

ROM work and talked to him about producing a catalogue for them in exchange for a full scholarship with room and board.

Then David heard about a new training and internship program, backed by a group of major Hollywood film studies. The program invited computer artists to submit a portfolio of their work to be considered for entrance. David did and was one of those chosen.

You see, as David found and developed his strengths, doors opened for him. And if you discover your child's talent and continue to believe in him no matter what obstacles he faces, you'll be amazed at what he can achieve and where these gifts take him. Every child has gifts—not just the children who are "stars" at academics or sports. A child may show promise in several areas, or his blending of intelligences may produce a unique ability. If recognized and encouraged, almost every child develops strengths in at least one particular area of "giftedness."[4]

HOW CAN YOU DISCOVER GIFTS?

Think about gifts, talents, and natural ability. What does your child do well? What does your child really enjoy doing? Don't look at only outward characteristics or at personality traits that make your child everybody's favorite.

I've found that even seemingly negative qualities in childhood are markers or signs of certain talents. For example, do you have a bossy child, one who orders around her friends—or maybe even *you* and siblings? This is the little child that you have to remind, "I'm the mommy, remember?" Bossiness in early life shows administrative talent, someone who, after developing maturity and people skills, could someday run a company or organization.

Or do you have an argumentative child, one who has a different opinion of the Noah and the Flood story and argues with the Sunday school teacher about it? This kid is always asking, "Well, why is that so? Who says so?" and seems to continually challenge what's being taught. Although this trait can be irritating, argumentativeness is the major sign of analytical intelligence—or what's called logical-mathematical talent—possessed by physicists, chemists, and others in the science field.

So take out some paper and list your child's positive and not-so-positive qualities, skills, and passions. If you're having a hard time thinking of talents, ask God for help in seeing these gifts and then look for ways to develop them. After all, he knows our kids best, because he made them! Sometimes we look at our children through the filter of our own disappointments or their previous failures and from time to time need the windshield of our vision cleaned off.

Whether your children like to tinker with computers, play the saxophone, fix lawnmowers, or write novels—accept and highlight those strengths. Focus on what they *can do* instead of what they *can't do*. Avoid squelching their enthusiasm with criticism like, "You aren't playing that piece on the guitar *again*!" or by asking, "What's *that?*" when a child shows you a sculpture made in art class. Instead, be enthusiastic about your children's projects and interests, even their early attempts at doing something.

Let them know that it's great to try new things and that they don't have to do them perfectly the first time. Encourage them to explore their interests and to be unafraid of making mistakes, to pursue the things they really have a passion about learning and doing, even if those things are different from what you like to do. If you do, you'll provide an environment where gifts and talents can bloom—some earlier and some later—and learning will be much more fun.

LESSON OF THE DAY

Help your children find their own strengths and develop them.

Be a Storytelling Family

Hearing and telling stories provides incredible benefits for a child's overall development and learning.

One of the best things I ever did for my communication skills was to take a graduate course in storytelling, sitting under the tutelage of the top tale spinners in our state. Why is storytelling so valuable? Besides the sheer joy and entertainment of storytelling, stories are the best method of transferring values from one generation to the next. Practicing and telling a story is terrific exercise for a child's memory and at the same time provides growth in creativity, language skills, attention span, and vocabulary. It's amazing that something with so many benefits costs so little—virtually nothing except the gift of time! That's why in today's lesson we're going to focus on fun ways to integrate storytelling into your interactions with your child.

SPINNING A YARN

You may be thinking, "Me—*tell* a story? I read them with my child, but storytelling is an art; you have to be a born storyteller!" That's what I used to think, but I discovered in the storytelling course that storytellers are made, not born. With some inside tips and a little practice, you can share the fun of a well-told story with your child and in the process help your child learn something from the experience.

Maybe, like my brother George, you have such a vivid imagination that you can spontaneously relate stories like his "Cowboy Bob" bedtime tales he told his boys Zack and Jonathan. Or my friend Kay, who could zip off episodes of "The Mysterious Bear" to the neighborhood kids while driving for the car pool every week. But there are some other easy ways to spin a yarn. Try these techniques:

- Tell a true story from your own experience. Think of a specific age and a time during that period of your life when you were the very happiest (like your first love at sixteen), saddest (perhaps the loss of a beloved pet or friend), or the most frightened (like when you got locked out of the house on a dark Halloween night and your parents were gone).

  Recall the sights, smells, tastes, sounds, and feelings of the experience. Review what was said in the situation. Was there some special insight or discovery you gained from the experience? Then, next time you're tucking your child in bed and she says, "Mom (or Dad) . . . read me a story," ask, "How would you like me to tell you one from when I was young?" Then let the story flow. No, it probably won't be perfect, but your child will be delighted at hearing a little of your "history"—especially if you were mischievous or got in a bit of trouble.

- Another easy story starter is to get out one of your old photo albums. One of those photos is likely to prime the pump and cause you to recall an experience. Maybe it's a picture of a memorable Christmas or of a family trip that ended in a hilarious mishap. When a story emerges from your memory, stop there and tell the story to your child—and don't forget to share the feelings, tastes, smells, and sights of the experience.

- Get a picture in your mind's eye of your first childhood home and what it looked like. Where was your bedroom? Who were the people who lived there with you? What visitors came to see the family? What kind of neighborhood was it in? As you draw a simple sketch or plan of where the rooms were to jog your memory, everywhere a story happened, put an *X*. Then while you show the sketch to your child, tell one of those stories.

STORIES TRAVEL FAR AND WIDE

Does your child have a favorite folktale? Maybe it was "Cinderella." Or "Babouska," a favorite tale that traveled all the way from Russia to the United States a long time ago. Kids are delighted to hear a folktale, whether it's an old familiar one or a story they've never heard before. They usually end up passing it on.

First, find a folktale in a book of your own or from a public library. Read it over several times, mentally outlining the main events in sequence and noting the primary characters and any repeated words. Then try to picture the story, by scenes, on the movie screen of your mind. (Professional storytellers say picturing the story by scenes helps them remember it better than anything else.)

Next, practice telling the story to yourself several times in the mirror, in the car while driving, or even to your dog. Tell it in your own words while "seeing" each scene. Try adding your own gestures, dialect, or props (like a musical instrument, hat, or stuffed animal) to enliven the story. Don't hesitate to add some emotion or humor—that's what makes the story fun to hear. Then relax, invite your kids to listen, and enjoy telling the story in your own unique style.

THE DAY MOM HAD TO HAVE HER STOMACH PUMPED

I love to sit around a campfire or story-sharing circle with kids and listen to their tales. One day when I was teaching a creative writing class at Chisholm Elementary School in Edmond, Oklahoma, I asked to hear a few family history stories from the students before they wrote. Katie, a fifth grader, told us of the time her mom accidentally drank kerosene from her brother's tent and had to have her stomach pumped. Then Tammy, ten years old, told us a story about her grandpa who, during the Great Depression, took a cow to college since he had no money to pay for his tuition. He hoped the dean of the college would accept the cow in lieu of his expenses, and it worked. Four years later, Tammy's granddad got his college degree.

Once they try it, most children enjoy being storytellers, so here are some ways to get your child to spin a yarn:

First, designate one chair as the storyteller's chair. Decorate it with crepe paper, shiny or red velvet fabric, or anything you can dream up. (Kids love special chairs for any purpose: a birthday chair for the birthday person to sit in at meals, an author's chair when reading their written poems and stories.) Then have a family storytelling time after dinner one night, with you leading the way, sitting in the storyteller's chair and sharing a lively story.

- You can ask, "Who wants to share a 'scar story'?" This is a story about one's first black eye, stitches, or memorable mishap. Then ask if others would like to share their "scar stories."

- Try a round-robin story game: One person begins the tale, the next person in a circle adds some more action and perhaps a new character, and then the story line passes to the next participant to develop the plot a little more, and on around the circle.

- Collect old hats for your child from garage sales and thrift shops or Grandma's attic. Hats stimulate dramatic play and are great story starters.

- The next time relatives are over, especially older ones, give your child a tape recorder with a blank tape and have your child ask Grandpa or Great Aunt Sue (or whoever likes to talk the most) to tell a story from the family or their own history while your child records it.

Whether it's a starry summer night in the backyard or a cold winter's night gathered around the fireplace with everybody cuddled in sleeping bags, storytelling time can provide some of the sweetest memories for any family. Be sure to provide positive feedback for the tale tellers and maybe a treat afterward. But don't feel you have to be sitting down to engage in storytelling—you can share stories anywhere: in the car while traveling, when your child is sick in bed and needs some TLC, or while waiting at the dentist's office.

While you share stories and listen to your child's stories, you'll be painlessly reinforcing some vital skills: creativity, memory, language, sequencing, comprehension, and word power, just to name a few. Are you ready? Let the story begin.

LESSON OF THE DAY

Storytelling is a powerful tool for learning, especially when parents model an enjoyment of it.

Boost Math Learning with Everyday Activities

Teach your children to use math to solve real-life problems and they'll discover that math can be fun.

How many of us have heard our children say, "I don't like math!" or even worse, "I'm dumb in math!"—and felt our own "math anxiety" rise up out of memories of tough trigonometry or algebra tests that threw us for a loop in high school? Or maybe you're like the majority of American parents who believe that only the few students who excel in and enjoy math have a "mathematical mind." Not so, according to new research.

A team of American and Asian scientists studied the reasons why Japanese and Chinese children outperform American students in mathematics. They discovered that the difference had less to do with superior teaching techniques or "mathematical minds" than the belief system of parents and teachers. Chinese and Japanese adults believe that the difference between failure and competence in math is due to hard work, and this belief encourages a positive attitude in students toward math.[1] Math educators in the United States agree, saying that most kids can learn and even enjoy math if they are properly motivated.

Let me encourage you with what Claudia Zaslavsky, author of *Preparing Young Children for Math*, says about this issue. It inspired me when I was helping my frustrated third grader master her multiplication tables:

"Some people say, 'I don't have a mind for math' but we know now that every person has a mind for math, provided the math is presented in an understandable manner. Research has shown that children of all ethnic backgrounds, girls as well as boys, are equally capable of learning mathematics."[2]

Armed with this hopeful information, I reminded Alison that *you can* when her mind-set was *I can't*. I showed her how to put the times tables on a blank tape so she could orally practice them, and made a game out of her multiplication flash cards for the daily practice she needed to memorize them. In time, the day came when it all clicked—and she had it!

So today let's look at how to help your children enjoy learning math, because the biggest obstacle or asset they'll bring into the classroom is their *attitude* toward mathematics. The key to a positive attitude is for your child to see that math has an important place in everyday life and to learn to use it to solve real-life problems. As you point out that numbers are everywhere and that we use them constantly, math will make more sense to your child and computing will be more natural in the classroom.

THE NUMBERS GAME

If you have a sports-minded child, call attention to strategy and plays in football and batting averages in baseball. You can even surprise your child by demonstrating that fractions are essential in most team sports. For example, if José, the batter, who hits "three for four" comes to bat and gets a hit, he'll now be "four for five." How does that compute in fractions? (4/5)

How does it look in decimals? (.800) How will José's performance in that game affect his season standing? As your child sees that batting averages are three-place decimals, math becomes something that's not a bunch of boring worksheets but actually might be interesting.

Our son, Chris, got so interested in sports statistics as a kid that he studied his favorite teams' stats every morning in the newspaper. He knew every player's batting average and every team's standing—and this interest carried over to his math achievement in the classroom.

What about travel? Every time your family embarks on a trip you have great opportunities for letting your child use math. Your child can use a map to determine how far it will be to your vacation destination, then help you figure the total cost of lodging, taking into account the difference between motel rates and camping fees. Your child can keep a record of gas fill-ups to figure miles per gallon: the total miles driven since the last fill-up, divided by the number of gallons purchased, will equal the miles per gallon that the car is getting. Keeping count of how far you have to go or how many license plates from different states you can find are all fun ways of using math while traveling. And in the process, your child will be discovering some useful math concepts.

The grocery store is another place your child can use math to solve real-life problems. Let your child clip coupons from newspapers and magazines and, using a pocket calculator, figure the amount of savings. When you go to the grocery store, have your child find the items that match the coupons. If you give your child half of all the money saved from the coupon shopping, you'll find this a *motivating* math activity.

TEACHABLE MATH MOMENTS

If you have younger children (preschool to early elementary age), they can learn math skills like categorizing, counting, measuring height, and comparing sizes and amounts in a hands-on way around the house. In the kitchen you can ask: "Which orange is bigger?" Count out cookies or grapes: "Here are your four cookies: one, two, three, four."

Another terrific math resource is a "Growth Chart" on the wall of your house or garage to measure and record the height of different members of the family. If you display the height in both inches and centimeters, then older kids will begin to understand the metric units of measure. Asking "Who is tallest—Dad, Mom, sister, or brother?" or "How many inches have you grown since Christmas?" gives practice in both comparing heights and subtraction.

Let your child sort laundry, blocks, and money (into stacks of quarters, dimes, nickels, and pennies). Also, while putting away knives, forks, and spoons from the dishwasher into their proper slots in the kitchen drawer, your child learns categorizing skills used in math. Even setting the table gives good math practice. "Let's count how many people we will have tonight for dinner, including our guests. Now can you get out the silverware and set the table?"

If you take advantage of opportunities like these to use numbers naturally and talk with your child, explaining how you are using math in your daily life (while cooking, measuring for sewing or building something, calculating your balance in the checkbook), you'll be developing a positive attitude and building a solid foundation for learning math.

A COACHING APPROACH

What if your child gets stuck in a difficult set of math problems or is saying, "I hate math"? Avoid creating an "out" by saying, "I hated math, too" or "I always did terrible in math—it's no surprise you aren't good at it!" That will just provide an excuse and undermine learning by reinforcing a negative spirit.

Instead of letting an obstacle become an excuse to quit, show your child how to do a similar problem and then suggest trying the troublesome one. If the way you're explaining how to solve the problem isn't working, use manipulatives, like beans to count into small muffin cups, or toy cars or small blocks. Or try drawing a picture or graph to make the problem more concrete. Ask questions to walk your child through each step of the problem: "What do you think we should try first? Okay, let's make up a simpler problem and see if that will work. Good, that should work here, too. Now what will we do next?"

Whenever you can, reinforce the math your children are studying in the classroom by having them teach you their newly learned skills and by finding ways to use those math skills in your daily life. If the teacher is introducing percentages, you could get your child to figure what percent of your weekly food money goes for dairy products. For older kids, use stock market prices to teach profit and loss, and baseball games to practice using decimals. As you look around, you'll find several ways to turn everyday chores into learning experiences by doing them with your child.

FUN AND GAMES

Last, remember that old saying, "All work and no play makes Jack a dull boy." By playing card games, children painlessly can build math skills. With a deck of cards they get opportunities to count, match suits and numbers, practice logic and problem solving, judge quantitative rank of numbers, and much more. For children with a learning disability, card games are especially helpful because they motivate them to work at something over and over again just because it's so much fun or so challenging.

In fact, Dr. Margie Golick, a child psychologist and specialist in helping children with learning disabilities, says that an inexpensive deck of cards is the best educational tool available to teach children essential math concepts. She worked with a first grader who still couldn't remember the difference between a "2" and a "6" or other numbers even after much instruction in school. He had attention problems and was spatially confused. After she taught him to play the card game Go Fish, and he played it for a week, he was able to master instant recognition of the numbers from 1 to 10.[3]

Dominoes, board games like Monopoly, and computer games are also good ways to learn and practice math skills while having fun. Let your children have a lemonade stand or help you with a garage sale, deciding how much to price items and keeping the profits from their own possessions or from the sale of lemonade. Making money and having a little Penny Power is of interest to most kids, and in the process they get excellent practice in managing money.

LESSON OF THE DAY

As you demonstrate the value of math skills in everyday life and give your child chances to use them, math will become more like a tool than a chore.

DAY 19

Develop a Close, Loving Relationship with Your Child

Relationship with parents is at the core of children's motivation for learning.

In these day-by-day lessons we've discovered some motivators for children's learning: having high expectations, boosting curiosity, focusing on the donut instead of the hole, teaching thinking skills and optimism, and tapping into their center of learning excitement—to name a few. But do you know the most powerful motivator for a child's brain development and learning? *It's your relationship with your child.*

How simple, how basic, yet how often we miss this. Kids need emotional warmth, caring, and unconditional love (which is spelled T-I-M-E) from parents. They need a close relationship with us and to know we believe in them no matter what. But in the fast-forward pace of family life in America and all the efforts at school reform, a loving, nurturing relationship is the one factor that's been left out of many children's lives—and the one most necessary to learning.

The most recent research on brain development underscores the value of the relationship between you and your child in regard to learning. These studies show that the growth of intelligence comes from spontaneous emotional interaction with caring adults, and those between parent and child are *the most stimulating and vital of all*, according to Dr. Stanley Greenspan, author of *The Growth of the Mind*.[1]

The vibrant personal involvement between parent and child is what gives rise to a child's ability to learn, wonder, and think about new ideas. When emotional needs are met at home, a youngster will have the mental energy needed to be enthusiastic about life and learning. Yet many of our nation's kids lack what they need most—parents' time and attention.

Children who have the assurance of being deeply loved and the security of feeling cared for by parents are "emotionally available" for learning. Those children can better focus on their studies and will retain more of what they learn. They also will form better connections with teachers, coaches, and other adults. Children are receptive to teachers' instruction in proportion to the degree that they have learned to care about the adults in their world. This kind of caring grows out of their own experiences of being cared about, respected, and loved at home.[2]

In contrast, when children lack a sense of emotional security because of a distant relationship with parents or turmoil at home, they tend to develop motivational problems—they could learn, but won't. And no expensive private school or high-tech learning programs can replace the need for a close parent-child connection. Even in the high school years, that relationship continues to be a key to healthy development.

Studies of teenagers who were learning, thriving, and had high goals and achievement records found that these teens were the ones whose parents stayed involved and engaged with them, not only in their early years but throughout high school.

What did these parents do? They did a great deal of talking with their kids and spent time with them. They didn't provide them with very much early freedom in dating and driving. They weren't harsh or overprotective, but established clear boundaries of behavior and showed a real interest in their children's lives, in school and out. Most important, they weren't too busy for their kids because they made parenting a high priority.[3]

HUGS AND LOVE AND "PAT THE BUNNY"

Have you ever felt as though you've read *Pat the Bunny* so many times to your child that you could say the words in your sleep? All that love and rocking, feeding, reading, and wiping noses and tears is part of relationship building with our kids in the early years. As John Drescher, one of the wisest voices I know in the parenting field, said, "The parent who holds the child during the early years will have a child who will hold the parents dear in later life."[4]

What about the elementary and middle years of our children's lives? Doing things together as a family—mealtime conversations, working together and doing projects, going on family trips and outings to the zoo, the park, museums, and libraries, is important—as is playing sports or doing hobbies together, taking time to work puzzles and play board games, riding bikes, reading aloud together, praying together, and attending church as a family. With simple but important interactions between you and your kids, without consciously thinking about it, you share your values, your ideas, your love and, most of all, yourself. All these build a sense of belonging and a close relationship.

In fact, research shows that children and teens who eat dinner conversing around the table with family and those who go to church with their parents have higher achievement and lower drug and alcohol use. Yet it's so easy to get out of touch with our kids in the middle years and beyond, isn't it? They become busier with school activities, sports, and friends. And we may be busier with our jobs, caring for younger children, and other responsibilities at church or in the community. But we must avoid getting disconnected in these important years. Here are some ways I've discovered to stay connected, whether your child is five or fifteen:

- *Discover a common interest:* What do you and your child enjoy doing together? It's easy to find things that kids like to do with you in the early years. Toddlers and preschoolers usually love doing almost anything with Mom or Dad: baking cookies, grocery shopping, cooking dinner, twirling around the room to music, folding laundry, walking the dog around the block. Even getting down on the floor together and engaging in a little pretend play, where both of you become make-believe characters, results in imaginative play, laughter, creativity, and enhanced language skills.

  As they grow, children's interests change. So does our time together with them. But there are still many activities that provide natural chances to talk, listen, and just be together. When you discover something you both share an interest in—something you do with your child not as a duty but because you can talk and share about it when you're together—then make time for it! It's a gold mine for relationship building.

  You see, children need "focused attention," which means undivided attention concentrated on the child or teenager in such a way that she feels loved, knows she is so valuable in her own right that she warrants her parents' "watchfulness, appreciation, and uncompromising regard."[5] This kind of attention—which consists of eye contact, physical affection, and listening—is what best fills up kids' emotional tanks.

But most young people don't want Mom and Dad to just sit there, look at them lovingly, and wait for them to talk. They want to *do something*. In most cases, communication flows most naturally out of time spent together in an enjoyable and interesting activity, whether it's simple and spontaneous or more planned.

Maybe it's throwing a baseball in the yard after school, making model rockets and flying them, fishing, playing musical instruments together, riding bikes, collecting and polishing rocks, or playing a game. Perhaps it's father and son having a standing "Pancake Date" on Saturday mornings, or daughter and Mom sewing together. Those shared activities are relationship builders.

• *Get on their turf:* What if, when your son enters eighth grade or your daughter becomes a thirteen-year-old who thinks she's grown up, suddenly they don't want to be seen at the mall with Mom's arm around them? It happens! Or maybe the activity you have been doing with your youngster, like building and interior decorating a dollhouse, starts feeling babyish to her and she loses interest?

Then it may take a little thought or creativity to build a bridge. One way to do this is to look for ways to get on your child's turf. By "turf" I mean your teen's territory— being involved in what your teen is into, even if it's not your favorite activity. For me, that meant shooting baskets in the driveway with my 6 feet 2 inch basketball player Chris on occasional after-school days. He's a quiet young man who'd think Mom had flipped her wig if I'd sat him down in front of me and said, "Let's have special time and talk about how you're feeling." But while tossing the ball in the hoop, he'd open up and talk about how school was going or how he did on the practice court that day. I almost always learned something I didn't know, sometimes how to make a better free throw, but usually something about Chris.

With our daughter, Alison, her turf was the art studio, the guitar, and sometimes The Gap. Driving her to the mall (or even better, having *her* drive) for a few minutes of looking for a new pair of inexpensive but unique earrings, then stopping for a cherry-limeade or pretzel, gave us an opportunity to share and talk.

Whatever your child enjoys or likes to do, be interested. Participate in some way. Find a bridge. Let your child know you're available and accessible to listen. Keep building your relationship. Stay tuned in. Don't get disconnected in the middle school and teen years. No matter how big your kids are, they need you!

LESSON OF THE DAY

One of the best ways to foster a love of learning in your child is to build a close, loving relationship.

Boost Creativity

Wherever your child's creativity shows itself, encourage it.

Creativity is one of the greatest gifts God has given us, and young children are loaded with it. Their questions, their imaginative stories, even kids' prayers reveal their creativity. Jenny, a little girl I know, knelt beside her bed one night and said, "Dear God, if you could just find some way to put vitamins in candy and ice cream instead of squash and broccoli, I'd be so happy!"

But as children grow, something happens to this quality. In our society, at the age of five, the vast majority of children measure high in creativity. But by the age of seven, the figure has dropped to 10 percent, whereas only 2 percent of adults are considered highly creative.[1]

What happens to all that creative potential? Part of the problem may be that, just as staying in the lines is often encouraged more than original drawing, so is over-scheduling kids with so many lessons and structured activities that they have little time to daydream or make believe. As parents and teachers, we could do a great deal more to foster creativity. When we spark their creativity, kids talents' bloom and their love for learning flourishes. Today let's focus on some easy ways to boost your child's creativity.

PROVIDE A CREATIVE ENVIRONMENT

Set up a center for creative activity and you'll find that when the raw materials of creativity are available, your children will draw and make things on a regular basis. Then you'll be less likely to hear whining complaints of "I'm bored" or have to buy something from Toys R Us to entertain them. They'll learn to make their own fun by using their creativity.

One of the best ways is to make a Creativity Kit. In a few sturdy plastic bins, put interesting, colorful, or unusual materials such as: colored pipe cleaners, egg cartons, pom-poms, glue, plastic foam trays, squares of felt and fabric, flexible tubes (like toilet paper rolls or mail tubes), buttons, seashells, a canister of clay, markers and a big sketch pad, and tissue paper in bright colors. With odds and ends like these available, your child can create a hodgepodge sculpture one day or a colorful drawing the next.

Garage sales are terrific places to pick up inexpensive craft materials such as colored beads, old puzzles, musical instruments, and even cameras so that kids can try their hand at photography and create their own scrapbook of memories. With a multicolored stamp pad and stamps with your child's name, animals, flowers, and other designs, your child can make stationery and create invitations and thank-you notes.

Kids need some space and time to create, pretend play, and experiment. A specially set-aside corner or niche for projects and art works well. A table in the garage might be needed for woodworking, building rockets, or dismantling and fixing (with Mom's or Dad's help, of course!) toasters and small appliances. Add generous doses of encouragement, appreciation, and the attitude that it's okay to make mistakes and that a creative mess is better than "tidy idleness," and you'll go a long way toward stirring up creativity in your kids.

When you suggest that your child draw or paint, instead of saying, "make your picture look like this," encourage your child to make something new. If, after your child creates something, you have no idea what it is, ask, "Could you tell me about what you've made?" instead of "What is *that?*"

I love the story of American artist Benjamin West that demonstrates how powerful parents' words are in encouraging creativity. One day West was left in charge of his little sister Sally. He found some bottles of colored ink and decided to paint Sally's portrait. While painting, he made a big mess in the kitchen. When his mother returned, patient mom that she was, she didn't yell about the mess. She picked up her son's "portrait" and said, "Why, it's Sally!" and rewarded his efforts with a kiss and her delight at his creativity. "My mother's kiss that day made me a painter," West later observed.[2]

CREATIVITY—WHAT IS IT?

Creativity" is the ability to produce original ideas in any field, and there are so many ways to be creative! Sometimes people think if they can't play music, write poems, or draw, they aren't creative. But our children, made in the image of the Creator, have the potential to be incredibly creative in their own field of study or pursuit.

Creativity does often refer to originality in painting and composing music; certainly it's seen in dance and the other fine arts. But creativity is also expressed in designing a totally new prosthesis that enables amputees to run, developing a cure for a disease, inventing a new product out of plastic, solving problems in the business world or in government. Each time someone creates a new recipe or resolves a relationship or management problem, that's being creative.

Even in athletics, there's room for originality. Once the conventional way for high jumpers to cross the bar was with a forward leap. But in the 1968 Olympics in Mexico City, an athlete named Dick Fosbury surprised the crowd with a creative approach to high jumping. Fosbury took several bounding steps, then lifted off the ground and in midair turned his back to the bar and cleared it. Besides setting a new Olympic record of 7 feet, 4 inches, his new leap, called the "Fosbury Flop," became the standard in high-jumping.

DEVELOPING CREATIVITY

Whatever your children's interests are, encourage them to undertake projects in that field, like writing original computer programs, creating art pieces, writing their own books, or inventing something—whether these projects relate to school or not. Help them find creative work to do in their special area.

For example, Sarah, a sixth grader, was fascinated with science and had looked forward to entering the school science fair. But her school decided not to hold the event. Her dad encouraged her to create her own project and enter it in the state science fair on her own. She jumped at the chance and ended up getting an award.

Your teen may want to design and make her own clothes or create new computer software. When your kids come up with ideas, you can support them by brainstorming, helping develop their ideas, or gathering materials. Saying "That's a great idea" or "Try it, see what happens" can encourage their creative thinking.

CREATIVE PROBLEM SOLVING

Albert Einstein, as a toddler, surprised his parents by asking them, "Why doesn't she have wheels?" the first time he saw his infant sister. He thought she'd be a toy and thus, like his other playthings, have wheels.[3] Creative thinkers ask interesting questions like: "How does the heart work?" "How was that skyscraper built?" For questions that don't have a "right" answer, let your child muse about the possibilities, do experiments, or research in books to discover more information.

One day Jared, a six-year-old, got lost in a department store at the mall. After his relieved and grateful parents found him, they used the experience to help him do some problem solving, talking with him about what his alternatives would be if he ever got lost at the state fair or grocery store. Then they used their imaginations and played a "What if?" game. They asked him: "What if you got lost on a desert island? What would you do? How about if you got lost on a giant cruise ship in the ocean?" "What if?" games are also great starters for writing stories and creating plays. In fact, that's one of the ways new movie scripts are developed: "What if aliens from outer space landed on earth and decided to take over Washington, D.C., and other major cities in the United States?"

Creative thinking and problem solving are important life skills. If your children develop creative thinking ability, they may go about a task in an innovative, fresh way. They may not necessarily make the very best test scores in class, but they'll be able to combine different experiences and ideas and see them in a new way, or look at an old problem and come up with a solution that's never been tried. This kind of original thinking is extremely valuable and, if developed, will help a person soar in achievement in post-college work such as graduate school, career, or ministry.

A FEW CREATIVITY-ENHANCING TIPS

If you want your child to develop creativity, be patient with starts and stops on projects. And be a role model by using your own imagination occasionally to have some fun together. One mom I know helps develop her four kids' imaginations by having special "pretend" days. One morning she'll say, "Today we're going to be pioneers. Let's dress as pioneers, and when we eat, we'll pretend we're in wagons." They don't use electricity on their pioneer day; they cook out on the patio, and the kids have great fun at little expense. On another day they'll imagine they're a family during a World War II bombing in England, and on another, they imagine they're on a spaceship together.

Be childlike and playful, maybe doing some finger painting together or having a pretend "Tea and Cookies Party" or getting on the floor in an old cowboy hat and pretending you're riding the range. Children love to imagine and, as they do, their creativity is being exercised. And you just might have some fun, too!

LESSON OF THE DAY

Creativity is a vital building block
for learning, problem solving, and
getting the most out of life.

DAY 21

Build Positive Momentum for Learning

Do whatever you can to get positive momentum going in the direction of learning, achievement, and motivation.

For most of us parents, spending a lot of time cheering at Little League games, swim meets, or soccer games while our kids play is part of the job description. One of the things I noticed when I spent time in the bleachers through my children's sports activities is how important *momentum* is to the outcome of the game. Our son's football coach once told the players how the game of life is much like football: You've got to block your fears, tackle your problems, and whenever you get the opportunity, head for the goal and *score all the points* you can. Since I love sports analogies, I added that one to my memory bank.

But the truth is that education and learning also are similar to football, especially in the area of momentum. I was reminded of this while watching the University of Oklahoma play Texas Christian University this fall with my son, Chris, and husband, Holmes. Being the home team, OU had a huge opening-game crowd filling the Sooner Stadium and a great new head coach hired from the Dallas Cowboys staff. The OU players were fired up to win!

However, in the first few minutes of the game, TCU got a quick field goal. Soon after, OU fumbled and TCU made a touchdown. They were hot. Their fans exploded. The OU players kept trying with all their might, but a few more fumbles derailed their efforts. With every yard TCU made toward the goal line, more momentum built until they had the upper hand and the game: final score 20 to 7.

Now what does that football game have to do with your child's learning? Let me explain. When the school year starts, whether you're home schooling or you've taken your child for the first big day with a new teacher, your child is at a starting point. Perhaps you both have expectations of a wonderful year of learning. If interesting projects spark your child's motivation, if the teacher takes an interest in your child and a good relationship builds, so does positive momentum for learning. But if your child is having a reading problem that makes every task grueling or if your child fails on assignments and tests, what happens? The wind goes out of your child's sails. A downhill spiral can begin and it negatively affects learning. To avoid that, today's lesson is going to focus on getting a good start, tackling any problems, and building positive momentum.

GET OFF TO A GOOD FIRST QUARTER

In anything, whether it's the beginning of a football game, a new job, or a school year, getting off on the right foot is important. One of the ways to help your children get a good "first quarter" is to have an opening pep talk, just as the coach does. After asking how your children feel about the year and what their expectations are, do some listening and maybe share about one of your first days at a new school or job.

You may want to give some suggestions like these: Explain how first impressions color your view of someone and that teachers tend to get some kind of an impression of their students during the first few weeks that will color their relationship with the children the rest of the year. You can help by meeting the teacher before school starts and letting the teacher know how you are involved in your child's education at home and what your expectations are for your child. When teachers know a child's parents and have a positive connection with them, that positively affects the way they deal with the student in the classroom. Momentum for learning increases a little more.

Encourage your children to sit relatively close to the front of the room to better hear directions and pay attention. Encourage them to ask questions when they don't understand something, to be interested and polite, to turn work in on time, and to stay tuned in to what's going on in class. Help them set up a daily study time to do homework right at the beginning—and it will make a world of difference throughout the rest of the year (as we discussed on Day 15). This doesn't mean that your children are apple-polishers who try to get in good with the teacher; it means they realize that having a good relationship and getting a good start will be to their advantage. Plus, they'll learn a great deal more, enjoy class more, and have a much better year.

If you will remember to look for something positive or helpful that the teacher does in the first month of school—perhaps a terrific science experiment that really interested your child or the way the teacher helped when your child was stuck in math—and write a note of appreciation or a thank-you for that specific action, you'll be adding to the positive momentum.

TACKLE THE PROBLEMS

What if your child has gotten a good start, is doing homework daily and trying hard, but gets hit by a problem with spelling or science or another academic area? Then tackle the problem! It's vital that you find out what the problem is and come up with a solution instead of allowing a negative label to be attached to your child. Instead of saying, "He has a math disability," for example, find out what your son doesn't understand in math, where the gaps are in skills, and help fill the holes. It might take a math educator at a local college or a retired math teacher to spend an hour with your child to assess what the problem is, but discover the problem and then tackle it with a solution.

If your child has a weakness or difficulty that is hindering learning in any subject, there are numerous possibilities to remedy the situation and get your child back on track. What's important is that you *help your child compensate for or bypass the weakness*. If it's a fine motor problem that makes handwriting difficult and slow, provide a laptop computer for writing notes and reports in the classroom. For students with low visual strengths, a colored transparency sheet in a rose or teal color to cover a page of print can reduce glare and enable them to read much better.

One student I worked with had trouble writing down directions and class notes due to some delays in fine motor skills development. So he took a small tape recorder to every class and tape-recorded teacher presentations and instructions for assignments, then reviewed them at home before doing his homework. He also had two textbooks on tape to listen to as he read. (Students with deficient reading levels can qualify for Books on Tape through the Library of Congress to aid their learning.) By using these compensating strategies, he became a motivated learner and a high achiever.

Be aware that when you or your child asks for a modification like one of these in the classroom, the purpose is to empower and equip your child to learn, not to take away responsibility or provide excuses for not doing the work.

If your child fails spelling tests, show your child how to use the five senses to study the words instead of just reading silently.

Encourage your child to say the word while looking at it, then say it while trying to "see" the word in her mind's eye. She can trace the word in the air while spelling it orally, write it on a big chalkboard, or trace it in sand on a cookie sheet. Show her how to use a word guide (a special, compact spelling dictionary) or the spell-check features on a computer, and remind her that many talented executives and doctors aren't great spellers but use some of the above ways to compensate.

MORE WAYS TO GET POSITIVE MOMENTUM

Momentum" refers to forward motion or impetus—the force behind an action. You can also try these momentum-building strategies if your child is having trouble learning:

- Have reading skills evaluated, preferably by someone outside the school system, and then find a reading specialist at a local college to give one-to-one instruction. Or try a systematic phonics program at home, checking to make sure your child learns to decode words and read fluently.

- If your child is having trouble in a particular subject, tutoring can be a lifesaver (and college students in that field or retired teachers often offer reasonable rates).

- Get a "Study Buddy," a student who is a little older than your child and whom your child looks up to. The "buddy" can come once a week, show how to get organized, and help your child study for tests.

- Find a way your child can use skills or strengths at school. An elementary student was struggling in school and becoming discouraged. After his mom talked to the teacher and told her some of the child's skills, the mom and teacher put their heads together. John was a good worker, even as a second grader, and he loved to help others. So he was put in charge of the Computer Lab. He had to come ten minutes early to take the covers off the computers, turn them on, and make sure the room was ready for students.

After school, John stayed for ten minutes to tidy the room, turn off the computers, and cover them. He never missed a day of his duties all year, and the faculty was so impressed by how responsible he was that they made him supervisor, with four kids under him, for the next year. Using his strengths built self-esteem and momentum for learning in all his subjects.

Finally, I hope that if your child needs to build positive momentum and motivation for learning, you'll review all twenty-one days of this book throughout your child's school days. In our three weeks together, we've looked at literally dozens of fun ideas to help your child love to learn. Use them, adapt them—they work!

Keep encouraging your children, focusing on the donut, not the hole. Build on your children's interests and develop their unique talents. Enjoy reading all kinds of books together, including stories of people who struggled in an area, then overcame obstacles and succeeded. Seize teachable moments and share in the wonder of the world around you.

Show your children that they can learn in different ways—by drawing diagrams and picture outlines, by listening to tapes and discussing, or by moving and doing hands-on activities. Keep believing in your children, share their enthusiasm for learning and life and, most of all, *enjoy* your children's growing-up years—they fly by so quickly!

LESSON OF THE DAY

Build positive momentum for learning and your child will become a lifelong learner, equipped to succeed in school and life.

NOTES

DAY 1: Have High Expectations

1. *Family Circle* (September 1, 1996).
2. Vonnette Bright, "Women Today" radio program, Campus Crusade for Christ Ministry.
3. Norman Vincent Peale, "The Stupendous Power of Hope," *Plus: The Magazine of Positive Thinking* (May 1995): 19–20.
4. Ibid, 20.

DAY 2: Boosting Your Child's Curiosity

1. Jane M. Healy, Ph.D., *How to Have Intelligent and Creative Conversations with Your Kids* (New York: Doubleday, 1992), 101, 106.

DAY 3: Teach Your Child to Study Smarter

1. Cheri Fuller, *Unlocking Your Child's Learning Potential* (Colorado Springs, Colo.: NavPress/Pinon Press, 1994).

DAY 4: Cultivate Conversation

1. J. Madeleine Nash, "Fertile Minds," *Time* (February 3, 1997), 54.
2. From an excerpt from Leo Buscaglia's book *Papa, My Father* (New York: Slack, 1989) as quoted in *Reader's Digest*, (September 1989), 79.

DAY 6: Tap Into the Mozart Effect

1. From an interview with Dr. Gordon Shaw, University of California, Irvine, concerning his research on music and preschoolers reported originally in the author's book *How to Grow a Young Music Lover* (Wheaton, Ill.: Harold Shaw, 1994), 12.
2. From "Music and Your Child," the American Music Conference, 1988.

DAY 7: Focus on the Donut, Not on the Hole

1. John Drescher, *Seven Things Children Need* (Scottsdale, Penn.: Herald Press, 1976), 94.

DAY 8: Teach Optimism

1. Dr. Martin Seligman's book *The Optimistic Child* is a great guide for parents on helping children face challenges, overcome negative attitudes, and argue against their own pessimistic thoughts. Some of the concepts in this chapter are adapted from a live presentation by Dr. Seligman on the need for parents to teach optimism to their children.

2. "Superachievers," *Family Circle* (September 1, 1996), 77.

3. Kathy Seal, "Unlock Your Child's Potential," *Family Circle* (September 1, 1996), 79.

DAY 10: Raise a Reader

1. If you want more information on what reading program is best for different learning styles, see my book *Unlocking Your Child's Learning Potential*, chapter 8, "How Learning Styles Impact Reading Skills" (Colorado Springs, Colo.: NavPress/Pinon Press, 1994).

DAY 11: Help Your Child Become a Lively Thinker

1. From an intelligence test by Robert Sternberg, a Yale psychology professor and expert on intelligence, in his book *Beyond IQ*.(New York: Cambridge University Press, 1984).

DAY 13: Help Your Child Develop a Sharper Memory

1. Carol Marshall and Kaye Johns, *Success Strategies for At-Risk Students: Center for Success in Learning* manual (Dallas: Center for Success in Learning, 1992), 3:26.

2. Dr. Michael L. Jones, *The Overnight Student* (Bellingham, Wash.: Louis, 1990). To obtain a copy, contact the publisher at (206) 647-3229 or write: Louis Publishing, 1105 Inverness Lane, Bellingham, WA 98226.

DAY 14: Teach Responsibility

1. Bonnie Runyan McCullough and Susan Walker Monson, *401 Ways to Get Your Kids to Work at Home* (New York: St. Martin's, 1981), vii.

DAY 15: Handling Homework

1. Cheri Fuller, *Helping Your Child Succeed in Public School* (Colorado Springs, Colo.: Focus on the Family, 1993), 116.

2. From an interview with Dr. Wanda Draper, professor of psychiatry at the University of Oklahoma College of Medicine and consultant to the Oklahoma School of Science and Mathematics.

3. Faith Clark, *Hassle-Free Homework* (New York: Doubleday, 1989), 41.

DAY 16: See That Your Child Succeeds at Something

1. Bodie and Jake Thoene, "Unscrambling the Possibilities," *Focus on the Family* (May/June 1996), 4–6.

2. Howard Gardner, *Frames of Mind: The Theory of Multiple Intelligence* (New York: Basic Books, 1983), 239, 386.

3. Anne Geddes, "Baby Sitters," *People* (September 30, 1996), 119.

4. Gardner, *Frames of Mind,* 239.

DAY 18: Boost Math Learning with Everyday Activities

1. Sheila Tobias, "Making the Most of School," *Family Circle* (September 1, 1988), 56.

2. Claudia Zaslavsky, *Preparing Young Children for Math: A Book of Games* (New York: Schocken, 1979), xii.

3. Margie Golick, *Deal Me In: The Use of Playing Cards in Teaching and Learning* (New York: Monarch, Simon and Schuster, 1981), 22.

DAY 19: Develop a Close, Loving Relationship with Your Child

1. From an interview with Dr. Stanley Greenspan.

2. Margie Golick, *Deal Me In* (New York: Monarch Press, Simon and Schuster, 1985), 4.

3. From an interview with Dr. Arthur Bodin, past president of the Division of Family Psychology of the American Psychological Association and a senior research fellow at the Mental Research Institute.

4. John Drescher, *When Your Child Is 6 to 12* (Intercourse, Penn.: Good Books, 1993), 11.

5. Ross Campbell, *How to Really Love Your Teenager* (Wheaton, Ill.: Victor, 1981), 31.

DAY 20: Boost Creativity

1. From interview with Dr. Wanda Draper.

2. Quoted in John Drescher, *Seven Things Children Need* (Scottdale, Penn.: Herald Press), 108.

3. Stephanie McPherson, *Ordinary Genius: The Story of Albert Einstein* (Minneapolis: Carolrhoda, 1995), 8–9.

We want to hear from you. Please send your comments about
this book to us in care of the address below. Thank you.

ZondervanPublishingHouse

Grand Rapids, Michigan 49530

http://www.zondervan.com